RED HEADED GEEK
BILLY C. WIRTZ

Red Headed Geek

Written by: Billy C Wirtz
Editor: Kitty Wilson
Layout: Tyler Nash
Cover Design: Shannon Mattiza

Published by: Holy Macro! Books, Box 82, Uniontown OH 44685, USA
Distributed by: Independent Publishers Group, Chicago, IL
First Printing: September 2012. Printed in USA
ISBN: 978-1-61547-014-3
LCCN: 2012944930

CONTENTS

ACKNOWLEDGEMENTS

There are several places in this book where I discuss the principle of "right place, right time." This book is the ultimate example of that.

Go to any bookstore, find the section titled "How to Be a Successful Writer," and I'll bet that not one of them will advise: "Hang out in a 24-hour drugstore and talk to the clerk in the checkout line." But that's exactly how it happened for me. I was sitting in the all-night Walgreens in Cocoa Beach, talking with Joanna Golden about a recent magazine article I had written. A gentleman in line turned and asked: "Are you a writer?" I replied that I was. He then asked: "Are you published?" Once again, affirmative. It was my turn, "Why?" He answered: "I'm a publisher."

Unfortunately, in today's cyber-world, anyone who contributes poetry to the "Little People for Constitutional Amendments" blog can (and often does) call themselves a writer. Likewise, anyone with enough bucks to get any of a few hundred printing companies to publish their 400-page treatise *The Secret Connection between Nostradamus and Michael Bolton* can call themselves a publisher. Fortunately for both of us at the Walgreens, neither of us was in that boat. We exchanged some emails, had a high-power luncheon at Papa Vito's Pizza, and eventually produced the book you now hold in your hand.

I could spend a good 10 pages on the people who deserve to be listed in this section, but I'll stick to the ones who played a direct part in helping me get this done. First and most obvious:

Bill Jelen, publisher of Holy Macro! Books. He has been an absolute joy to work with, his checks have all cleared, and I hope this is only the beginning for both of us. Along with Bill, the other members of the Macro! empire: Tyler Nash, Scott Pierson,

Kitty Wilson for copy editing, and Shannon Mattiza for the way cool cover design.

Ted and Claudine Wirths, without whom I wouldn't be here.

David Wirths, the best brother a guy could ever wish for.

The Fabulous Moolah, for all the encouragement.

Katie Glass, my teenie weenie meanie.

Bob Doershuk and John Bordsen, my two mentors, the guys who taught me the finer points of the writing craft.

Joanna Golden, for putting me in the right place at the right time.

Dr. Russell Meetze, the man who saved my life.

Mickie Jay, Steve Keirn, Mike Graham, Diamond Dallas Page, Sir Oliver Humperdink, and Tim Parker, my brothers in the wrestling business.

Ken Coble, my dear friend, adopted brother, and technical advisor to this volume.

And now for everyone else, in no particular order of importance, but equally vital to the completion of this project:

Harold, Victor, Mardi, Roger, Judith K., Judith L., SideShow Bennie, Harry T., James T., Tommy D., Fast Eddie, Bob, Warren, Bird, Linda Sue, Larry and Bruce at Hightone, Amy, Hossman Allen, John Swain, and the staff at WFIT, KPIG, and WNCW.

A special thanks to Papa Vito's Pizza in Cocoa Beach, where the deal was struck.

My eternal thanks to each and every one of you. My apologies to those of you I didn't name here, but you know who you are.

I wish I could take credit for the following story, but it was told to me years ago by one my best friends, Aaron Cross. I could waste a lot of words discussing the attitudes of the public about wrestling, but this pretty well sums it up and makes for a good starting point. Buckle your seat belts.

Back when I was in high school, I ran around with what my mom called a "rough crowd." Prominent in this group were Jack Moore and Wynn Thompson. They were both thick, burly fellas, very strong. But in other ways, they were quite different from each other. Wynn was mild-mannered, kind of quiet, and, despite his carousing, a gentleman. Jack— or Jolly Jack, as he was known—was also laid back . . . when he was sober. Get him drunk, and in his own words, he was "the proverbial bull in a china shop."

One day Wynn's parents were out of town, so we "borrowed" his dad's VW bus and rode around a wooded section of town, drinking Schlitz malt liquor out of 8-ounce cans and chasing it with Ripple.

Jack was riding shotgun, and as all guys who ride shotgun do from time to time, he spat out the window. Unfortunately, in his Schlitz/Ripple-altered state of consciousness, he didn't notice that the window in question was still in the up position, so he landed a big one onto the glass. This upset Wynn—it was his dad's car, after all—and he told Jack to clean it up. Jack just grinned and spit again. Wynn told him to stop, Jack spit again, again Wynn told him to stop, and this time Jack hit the window with his fist. It shattered.

Wynn pulled the car into the woods and stopped. He

got out, Jack got out, and the rest of us did, too. It wasn't merely going to be a fight, but a battle royal between two bruisers. Wynn was steaming mad, but he just somehow couldn't throw the first punch, so he got into Jack's face and started talking smack about his mama. Jack just spit again—and grinned. Wynn started talking bad about Jack's car. Again, nothing from Jack but more spitting and grinning. After a moment of deliberation, Wynn leaned in and slowly whispered, "Wrestling's fake."

It was on.

HEY, BOY!

"Hey, boy!"

I was strutting back from the ring, having just completed my first night as a professional wrestling manager. I looked up just in time to see a large black fist coming toward me.

The next thing I remember, I was being pulled into the dressing room. Someone was handing me an icepack to help relieve the throbbing sensation now spreading across the left side of my face. As my eyes began to focus, I became aware of a roomful of professional wrestlers applauding and congratulating me.

One of them pointed to the door; on the other side of it, the corrugated steel walls reverberated with the sound of 200 delirious wrestling fans chanting "Red Headed Geek." My boss, Steve Keirn, stuck out his hand and said, "Way to go, Reverend. They really hate you. You're doing great!"

"YOU WANT TO BE A WHAT?"

1 WHY I WROTE THIS BOOK ... AND SOME THOUGHTS ON WRESTLING

When I began writing this book, I thought I'd tell a few wrestling stories, reveal a few insider tidbits, and maybe even convince a few nonbelievers that there is indeed a degree of authenticity and importance to professional wrestling.

I went to the local chain bookstore, and not only were there at least two dozen "tell-all" bios by wrestlers, there were several written by wrestlers' wives, one or two by wrestlers' therapists, and even a new-age self-help book written by the infamous Bobby "The Brain" Heenan.

Does anyone read wrestling books? Doesn't pro wrestling appeal primarily to rednecks and the less educated? Isn't this the same bunch that believes Elvis is alive? The answer to all three questions may be *yes*, but there are a couple other kinds of wrestling devotees, who fall into two main groups: what I call "smart" fans and "in-the-closet" fans. Then there are the skeptics.

"Smart" fans are aware that the outcome of a wrestling event may be predetermined but enjoy the show anyway. These fans include English professors, tax lawyers, jazz musicians, elected officials, and virtually anyone with a B.S. in something. Newsletters are written for these fans, foremost among them *The Wrestling Observer*, published and written by Dave Meltzer. The Observer is a brilliant piece of journalism. It was one of the first publications to "expose" inside secrets of the business. Meltzer uses insider terms—you'll learn more about those later—and he's a damn fine writer. He's also highly opinionated. Even though they pretend not to care, the wrestlers read every single word of the Observer, often making career-changing decisions based on what Meltzer reports.

I'm willing to bet that within hours after the first porno website was launched, some "smart" fan started a wrestling site. Of all the . . .

The second easily identifiable group of wrestling fans are those who just can't quite come out of the wrestling closet. These are the ones who, in the middle of a Vietnamese restaurant, will look across their bowl of pho and ask me, "Didn't you used to be a wrestler or something?" When I explain that I was indeed involved with the wrestling business, there is an inevitable pause, and then, "I used to watch that stuff as a kid. It's all fake, right?"

Well, yes, for the most part, the outcome of an individual match is predetermined. However, really great wrestlers have the ability to make even the most cynical pause and say "Gee, that looked kind of real." Just like in any other sport, there are good wrestlers, and there are great wrestlers. The difference lies in the wrestlers' ability to suspend your disbelief. And that suspension of disbelief is necessary to sell tickets, especially to the general public, most of whom qualify as skeptics.

There's almost nothing better than converting a skeptic into a fan. I'll bring a friend or two, if they'll promise to keep an open mind and respect the "less enlightened" fans around us. It usually takes a match or two to for them to lose their agnostic detachment.

The transformational moment usually occurs around the third bout. The ref has his back turned, and the bad guy seizes the moment to deliver an illegal kick to the solar plexus, knocking the good guy out of the ring. When the good guy hits the floor with a resounding thud, my friends say something like, "Wow, that had to hurt a little." When the evil manager sneaks up and delivers a karate chop to the windpipe, leaving the hapless hero gasping for breath, they'll mutter, "Hey, that's not cool." The bad guy and his manager gang up on the good guy, hurling him out of the ring and through the scorekeepers' table with a violent crash. When he gets up, he's bleeding profusely from a nasty forehead wound.

Suddenly, my friends are yelling at the bad guy, and I have to remind them that this is a family show, and there are some, albeit minimal, verbal boundaries.

By the end of the night, along with a dozen new friends they've made in the surrounding seats, my new converts are standing on their chairs, screaming themselves hoarse during the main event: a brutal cage match that ends with one of the participants being taken out on a stretcher. All the folks I take to the matches, even the most staunch skeptics, thank me and express a desire to go with me the next time. And it's all because the wrestlers can make the audience suspend their disbelief. In this book, I hope I can shed some light on a few of the incredibly complex psychological tactics I have both witnessed and learned to suspend that disbelief.

2 RASSLIN' 101

The following is by no means a complete history of the wrestling business. It's a quick overview of its origins, followed by a couple of items you should be aware of.

In the Beginning

Professional wrestling began on the backroads of America in the late 1900s. It began as a carnival attraction, challenging local toughs to try their luck in a three-sided makeshift ring.

A designated "champion" would offer to take on all comers, challenging them to stay in the ring for a given period of time—usually three short rounds. If the challenger succeeded, he would win $25, but of course that never happened. Instead, the alcohol- and testosterone-bloated "mark" would have barely stepped into the ring before the champ had him in a painful leg- or arm-lock, and the match usually ended in less than a minute.

On rare occasions, the rube would gain the upper hand. When that happened, the champ would work him into a corner, and behind the corner was a curtain. Behind the curtain, a black-jack-wielding carnie ensured victory for the champ.

As we will see later on, wrestling owes a major debt to carnivals and carnies. The dominant underlying mindset of old-school wrestling evolved directly from the sideshow.

The Early Days

The first championship match for a world title was held at Chicago's Dexter Park Pavilion in 1908, between Frank Gotch and George "The Russian Lion" Hackenschmidt. Gotch won on a disqualification after a brutal 2 hours and 3 minutes. For the next decade or so, wrestling drew big crowds. But then fans got tired of seeing 30-minute headlocks, and attendance waned.

In the mid-1920s, a shrewd promoter, Toots Mondt, introduced time limits on all matches. He also added excitement with such moves as the flying dropkick. And he gave wrestling its first genuine superstar: Ed "Strangler" Lewis. Lewis hardly looked the part. He was balding and had a constantly expanding beer gut and pencil-thin legs. But he fought a total of 6,200 legit "shoot" matches and won all but 13 of them.

Over the next two decades, wrestling's popularity rose and fell. But it never really caught on with the general public until the advent of television. Television boosted professional wrestling's popularity as both spectator sport and morality theatre. Later in this book, I'll fill you in on the changes that occurred in the late 1980s and early 1990s, but now I have an obligation to make you aware of two very significant events in the history of wrestling that were responsible for major changes in American culture. The first one happened in the early 1950s.

The Human Orchid: Gorgeous George

When cultural historians recount the early years of television, there's universal agreement on its first major celebrities: Milton Berle, Ernie Kovacs, and Elvis all sold the public on television. But the man responsible for actually selling more TVs than all the others combined was a Nebraskan named George Wagner, a.k.a. Gorgeous George, a.k.a. The Human Orchid. Some even think that Gorgeous George is the person who propelled television toward becoming the entertainment medium it is today.

Gorgeous George established a character now considered a staple of wrestling. He bleached his hair platinum blonde and wore spectacular ornate robes. He always entered the ring to the strains of "Pomp and Circumstance," his valet spraying the mat with Chanel #10 as George tossed gold "Georgie Pins" to the audience. Gorgeous George was really a great wrestler, but he knew that his athletic skills alone didn't sell tickets. He filled stadiums as "the guy you love to hate." His credo, and formula for success, was simple: "Win if you can, lose if you must, but always cheat!"

Gorgeous George not only revolutionized television and the wrestling business, he left his mark in several areas of sports and entertainment. Bob Dylan recalled meeting him early in his career and being totally mesmerized by The Gorgeous One. But perhaps the two most famous figures he influenced were a boxer and an R&B singer.

"Always Be Outrageous"

Back before he defeated Sonny Liston, Cassius Clay was fighting in Las Vegas. He was interviewed on a local sports radio show, and taking a stylistic cue from then-champion Floyd Patterson, he acknowledged the other fighter's abilities and promised a good clean fight. Gorgeous George was interviewed next. Barely had the announcer said his name before George went totally berserk, claiming that if his opponent, Freddie Blassie, beat him, "I'll crawl across the ring and cut my hair off! But that's not gonna happen because I'm the greatest wrestler in the world!"

After the interview, George advised the young boxer: "A lot of people will pay to see someone shut your mouth. So keep on bragging, keep on sassing and always be outrageous." The next night, Clay drew around 700 fans, while George packed in close to 12,000. After that, Clay changed his interview style.

The Capes

Long before he attained worldwide fame as "The Godfather of Soul," James Brown and his band were sitting in a motel room after a midweek gig somewhere in rural Georgia. The television in the room was tuned to wrestling. Gorgeous George was featured in the main event.

Brown and company watched in awe as once again a sold-out crowd at LA's Shrine Auditorium came close to rioting as a result of the blonde bombshell's antics. As usual, George had been disqualified for cheating. The referee kept trying to put a succession of his robes on him, only to have The Human Orchid throw the garments off and become more enraged with each attempt. The fans were at the boiling point, hurling insults, paper cups, and beer bottles at the ring.

The next night, during "Please, Please, Please," his closing song, James began to walk off stage; and as a joke, one of the Famous Flames threw a jacket around him. The small-town crowd went crazy as James threw the jacket off and came back to the microphone, falling on his knees and pleading, "Don't leave me, baby, don't leave me!" By the next week, it had progressed to a couple of jackets, and it soon became the most spectacular closing routine in popular music. Some nights there were with three capes, some nights four, and on special occasions, a spectacular fifth one. Every night for the next 40 years, James Brown ended every single show with "the capes."

Wrestling Loses a Legend

Gorgeous George retired from wrestling in 1962. His life after wrestling was not a very happy one. There were some bad business investments, and he fought a lifelong battle with booze until his passing on December 26, 1963, at the age of 48. Without him, both Muhammad Ali and James Brown might have evolved entirely differently. About the same time that George was influencing these stars, wrestling instigated a quiet but even more profound change in Memphis, Tennessee.

Wrestling Integrates Memphis

Memphis, Tennessee, was known for its terrible racial strife. Dr. King's death was only one event in the city's long history of racial disharmony and brutality. The first public event to allow open nonsegregated seating was not a church service or a political rally. It was Monday Night Wrestling at The Mid-South Coliseum. And the change occurred as a result of an ultimatum delivered by a professional wrestler.

For over two decades, Sputnik Monroe was *the* major wrestling star in Memphis. In the movie *Memphis Heat*, he explains that he was harassed by police and fined for drinking in bars on Beale Street with his black friends. Finally, he had enough. He was tired of being harassed, and he was tired of black wrestling fans being confined to the stuffy, overcrowded second-story "peanut gallery" during matches. He went to the promoter and told him that unless blacks were allowed to sit on the main floor at the coliseum with the other customers, he wasn't going to wrestle. At the time, Monroe was one of the top-drawing wrestlers, and to lose him would have been financial suicide for the promoters. There was a major uproar, but Monroe held his ground. The promoters changed the seating policy to "first come, first served."

Shortly after they interview Monroe in *Memphis Heat*, they interview an older black wrestling fan. His eyes well up as he recalls, "Man, oh man, you don't have any idea how proud he made us." He adds, "There was a time you could go into any black home in Memphis, and there would be three pictures: Jesus, Dr. Martin Luther King, and my man, Sputnik Monroe."

3 A CAST OF CHARACTERS

Numerous folks were important parts of my life during my tenure with the PWC and the WCW. Some of them are still among us, and others have gone on to that great cage match in the sky. Here I'd like to introduce you to a few of them. There have been dozens of others, and I could write a book just about the characters I've met in Waffle Houses along the highways. But for now, "Ladies and gentlemen, and wrestling fans of all ages, please welcome tonight's participants."

Lillian Ellison, a.k.a. The Fabulous Moolah

Without Lillian's help, whole episodes in my life might never have happened. She approved the idea for the video for my song "Teenie Weenie Meanie," and simply being associated with her opened many doors for me. She was a guiding force; whenever I called, she treated me like a favorite grandson. When it came to business, however, she was, in the words of all the old-school wrestlers, "one tough old broad."

Lillian was tough indeed. She had been in the business since the late 1940s. She took the name Moolah because, according to her, the moolah was what it was all about. In case there was any doubt about that, she sported a diamond-encrusted dollar sign around her neck as a reminder.

Lillian came to several of my music shows, and I remember one in particular. I was playing in Columbia, South Carolina, 50 miles from my home in Aiken and 20 miles from her home in Irmo. Naturally, people in the crowd stared, as this extremely well-dressed senior walked in with an equally well-dressed little person. The sight of her and Katie together made quite the visual impact. She sat quietly and demurely through my show. At the very end, I announced, "Ladies and gentlemen, we are in the presence of true royalty. Please welcome, along with her protégé, Diamond Lil, the queen of women's wresting, The Fabulous Moolah." The crowd of around 200 inebriated South Carolinians erupted. Moolah stood up and dropped into character, raising her arms like she'd just been introduced by a ring announcer. After the show, there was a line of about 20 people waiting for my autograph. A group of no less than 50, including bartenders, waitresses, and even the security guards clustered around her table.

Lillian truly had a heart of gold, but she didn't take crap from any human being on the planet. Showing me a scar on her leg one time, she said, "Some jerk burned me with a damn cigar on the way to the ring one night in Columbus, Georgia. I jumped over the guard rail, and I heard that he finally got out of the hospital a week later." She claimed to have dated both Hank Williams and Elvis.

During the shooting of the "Teenie Weenie Meanie" video, I told her about my wish to become a manager, and she strongly encouraged me, saying, "You've got the gift of gab." But then, in a most maternal manner, she cautioned, "Just don't let 'em blade you, sugar." (Stay tuned; I'll explain blading in Chapter 8.)

Page Falkenberg, a.k.a. Diamond Dallas Page

Diamond Dallas Page, or DDP as he referred to himself, is the ultimate self-motivated individual. The first day we met, he told me, "I am going to be a somebody, one way or the other." It was not merely a mantra; he spent all day, every day spreading the name and reputation of DDP just a little bit further. When we first worked together, he was moonlighting as a bouncer at a "gentleman's club" in Fort Myers, Florida.

After the PWF folded, DDP moved to Atlanta and, at the advanced age of 35, traded in his announcer's microphone for a pair of wrestling boots. He enrolled in wrestling school and spent 8 to 10 hours a day taking bumps from guys half his age. Then he'd go home and spend hours going over tapes of himself, making notes of moves and techniques that needed improvement. They started him off as a glorified jobber, but he never complained. Within five years, he won the World Championship belt. He also developed a great finishing move, "the diamond cutter," and the catchphrase "BANG!" to go along with it.

I've never seen a more tireless self-promoter; DDP radiates charisma, and it's genuine. You can't help but like him. When injuries forced him out of wrestling, without missing a beat, he began working the motivational speaker circuit and developed a program called YRG—Yoga for Regular Guys. He still runs this program, complete with a weekly podcast. He was major help to me during my stints with the PWF and the WCW, and he's one hell of a great friend.

Sir Oliver Humperdink

Sir Oliver Humperdink, or "Hump," as we knew him, was both a wrestling legend and a major music fan. The first day I walked into the PWF offices, he was sitting shirtless behind a desk reading *Mad* magazine. He was a natural redhead with the world's longest mullet and a full red beard to match. He was stocky and smaller in height than most of the other wrestlers, but he had a presence that lit up a room. Imagine a hobbit-like figure with multiple body piercings, attired in an unbuttoned Hawaiian shirt . . . that pretty well describes him. We stayed in touch from the time I broke into the business until he passed away from cancer in 2011.

One of the great managers in the business, Hump acquired a whole lot of ring wisdom during his four decades as the quintessential "heel." Hump taught me how to get heat from a crowd. He also taught me more subtle but highly important skills, such as knowing when to back off and let the wrestlers build excitement in a match and how to ignore the taunts from the audience for the first few minutes but then raise their collective tempers to the boiling point by commanding them, "shut your ignorant mouths!"

After Hump retired from the business, whenever I was in his hometown of Minneapolis, he came to every one of my music shows and was always a perfect gentleman to fans and admirers. Hump was a real class act and a truly inspiring mentor.

Mike Graham

Mike was the son of the legendary Eddie Graham. His father *was* Florida wrestling, establishing a multi-decade dynasty that produced some of the biggest stars in the business. Mike himself was maybe half the size of most of the other wrestlers, but he was afraid of no one, the most fearless human being I've ever known. He was also, along with Steve Keirn, the most loyal employer I've ever had.

Five years after I'd left the PWF, Mike and Steve arranged for me to get an audition with the WCW. Then, four years after that, they landed me a job writing the script for a famous feud involving Jay Leno and Hulk Hogan, which resulted in my first national TV exposure.

Steve "Gator" Keirn

Steve Keirn has been in the wrestling business for over 40 years, involved from every angle. At one time, he was part of a tag team, The Fabulous Ones, along with Stan Lane. They were some of the top drawing cards in the Memphis territory for much of the 1970s and 1980s. Legend has it that in the days before cable, they could sell 10,000 seats on a Monday night at The Mid-South Coliseum in Memphis.

When I worked with Steve, he was, along with Mike Graham, the boss of the PWF. As I mentioned before, both he and Mike continued to help me out even after I no longer worked for them. To this day, I am humbled by the generosity they've shown me.

Blackjack Mulligan

Blackjack was a true superstar in the wrestling business. He was 6′6″ and weighed in at around 275 pounds. He was in his 40s by the time I worked with him but still commanded respect from all the wrestlers. He'd been in wrestling since the 1950s and had two sons and a daughter who had followed him into the business. His finishing move was the dreaded "claw hold," and after shaking hands with him, I had very little doubt as to its legitimacy. He was a great friend and my primary teacher on how to cut promos.

Tim Parker and Al Greene

Tim Parker and Al Greene, a.k.a. The Bounty Hunters, were my main tag team. There are clips of me floating around on YouTube, and most of them involve me and The Bounty Hunters giving heat to any and all who dared cross our paths.

Al was a body builder and one of the strongest human beings I've ever known. Tim wasn't far behind. He wasn't as tall as Al, but he more than compensated for it in sheer strength and quickness in the ring. We had some great matches, and Tim now runs a computer repair service about three blocks from my house.

"Gigolo" Jimmy Backlund

Jim was a young, flashy wrestler with a lot of potential. We worked on developing his character—a strutting narcissist, a total show-off. It worked real well. He actually made it to the WWE and did quite well in the business until injuries forced his early retirement.

Mickie Jay

Of all the people in the wrestling business, I think I admire Mickie Jay the most. It's incredibly difficult to break into the wrestling business, but Mickie is, like DDP, an amazing example of doing whatever it takes.

Mickie Jay was a high school custodian who dreamed of working in the pro wrestling business. Although he wasn't big enough to be a featured "talent," he did virtually everything else one could do. He answered phones in the office, and he drove hundreds of miles to set up the ring for house shows. He was our designated referee, and not just any referee, either. He took some truly nasty bumps from the heels; I saw him bleed on several occasions. He also filled in as a jobber with both the WCW and WWE, taking brutal finishes and never complaining. He worked for extended periods of time with both the WCW and WWE, until certain medical tests (the ones that we all dread the most) came back positive.

Ever the fighter, Mickie refused to let cancer beat him, and at this writing, he's cancer-free and hanging out in sunny Key West, Florida. We still keep in touch, and he's been a major help in getting this book written.

Katie Glass, a.k.a. Diamond Lil

When I sat down and wrote the song "Teenie Weenie Meanie" at a friend's piano back around 1985, in Harrisonburg, Virginia, I had no idea it would change my life. But it did. Without Katie's help and top-flight performance in the video, none of this would have been possible. Thanks, Katie. You will always be the belt-holder of my heart.

4 PARTS UNKNOWN

Aiken, South Carolina
April 1959

> *Dear Mildred,*
>
> *Don't know if you've heard the latest, but apparently Bill caused quite a stir at St. Thaddeus Episcopal Church last Sunday. As you may know, every third Sunday of the month, they pick one of the children to lead the Lord's Prayer. This Sunday it was William's turn. He marched up to the front of the church, seemingly without a bit of fear. Adjusting his favorite little madras bow-tie, he began: "Our Father . . . " and then suddenly in an outburst of four-year-old dramatics, dropped to his knees, finishing the prayer with a commanding "Amen." The congregation burst into applause as he marched back to his front-row pew. Apparently, our son has a flair for the dramatic. Makes you wonder what he'll be when he grows up.*
>
> *Much love,*
> *Claudine*

If only my mother had known how prophetic those words were. Some people are ashamed to admit it, but I'm not: I love an audience. From the age of four rights up until this morning at the local coffee house, I've always loved to entertain people. Without analyzing it too much, I don't think it comes from a deep-seated inferiority complex or a constant need for attention as much as it does from a desire to see people happy. Being raised in a police station (my mother was a police psychologist and youth worker at one time in her life), I saw my share of sadness and suffering at an early age. I also saw happiness on the faces of people when someone was taking their mind off their troubles for a few minutes.

I've played music for 30 years, but I consider myself more of an entertainer than a musician. A true musician doesn't need an audience but is perfectly happy to sit and play for hours all alone. I enjoy sitting at home and playing old hillbilly songs on the piano, but there's nothing like the buzz I get from working a really good crowd.

From Aiken to D.C.

I was born on September 28, 1954, in Aiken, South Carolina. Life was simple and uncomplicated. I lived for Saturday mornings.

In Aiken, if you were under age 10, Saturday mornings meant one thing: "Bwana John and Tarzan." Bwana John was actually John Radeck, sales manager for station WJBF, Channel 6 from nearby Augusta, Georgia. But to us, he was our pith-helmeted guide to the world of Tarzan and such exotic foes as the Leopard People and the Amazons. Not only did he show Tarzan movies, he also ran contests, the most memorable being the Tarzan yell contest. I don't remember what the prizes were, but who could forget a stream of young Carolinians doing their nasal southern drawling best to imitate "AAAHH-AAAEE-AAHH-AAHH-EE-AAHHH"?

I guess that in some ways, the basic plot of every Tarzan movie was similar to the basic premise of pro wrestling: The good guy (Tarzan) is pitted against a bizarre bad guy (the Leopard People). The match (movie) begins, it looks like an easy win, for a while it looks like evil will triumph, but in the end the good-guy wrestler (Tarzan) triumphs.

At age 7, my world changed. We moved to Rockville, Maryland, a suburb of Washington, D.C., that was exploding with transplants from all over the country. We moved into a townhouse in a neighborhood known as Rollins Park. On one side of the busy main street were split-level townhomes, and on the other side there were three-story apartment buildings.

The neighborhood itself was a crazy-quilt of different cultures. Seventy percent of the families were Jewish, most of them from the New York area. At first, I was scared of them. They were loud, pushy, and aggressive. Their kids excelled in school and were fiercely competitive on the playground. Eventually, though, as kids do, we found common areas of interest. Back then, the most popular game was "playing army." Playing army necessitated having several guys on your side and ignoring religious affiliations. There were also learning opportunities. Coming from a southern town with one Jewish family, I knew nothing about Jewish customs and holidays. Within six months of moving to Rockville, all my playmates were Jewish. I can still remember my shock when Geoff Barnes told me he didn't celebrate Christmas—and my envy when explained that Hanukkah lasts eight days.

Back in the early 1960s, America was on a roll: Kennedy was president, young people were attending college in record numbers, the space program was in full swing, and even at our age, schools were preparing students to be upstanding members of American society. Virtually every aspect of our young lives was enhanced with life lessons. Sports and sportsmanship were considered to be as important to our proper growth and development as academics. Even if the local Catholic school had just demolished our Cub Scouts team in softball (which they always did), we were expected to conduct ourselves with a certain decorum. No matter how much we secretly hoped that every one of those guys had a grandmother who kissed them on the mouth, at the end of every game, we were expected to form a circle and chant: "Two, four, six, eight, who do we appreciate?" "Saint Whatever's!" followed by a loud group cheer.

This sportsmanship mindset carried over into the mass media as well. Baseball players were the quintessential role models. We idolized Mickey Mantle, Willie Mays, and Sandy Koufax with a fervor bordering on the religious. It was the era Floyd Patterson, a boxer who actually helped his opponents to their feet after knocking them out.

From Tarzan to Pro Wrestling

Somewhere in the excitement of new friends, new adventures, and new discoveries, I stumbled upon professional wrestling. At first I was stunned. Coexisting with the all-American, one-for-all mindset were grown men wearing outlandish clothes and flagrantly bragging to the announcer about how they were going to demolish their opponents. "Two, four, six, eight" indeed.

Wrestling was a real-life version of a Tarzan movie. In place of Johnny Weissmuller, there was a new cast of clean-cut heroes fighting a never-ending battle against Germans, blonde fat guys, and human giants. My parents tried to tell me professional wrestling was lowbrow, staged, and not to be held in the same esteem as "real" sports. They even attempted to bribe me into not watching it. In fact, my mother bought me a three-record set called "Shakespeare for Young People" and suggested that I listen to that instead of watching grown men hit each other with "foreign objects" and, in general, negate every rule of fair play we were being indoctrinated with. It was no use, I was hooked.

My first wrestling heroes were two Latinos: Cyclone Soto and Argentino Apollo. Unfortunately, they were both "jobbers," which means they got the tar beat out of them on a weekly basis. There were three main bad guys who used them for target practice: Dr. Jerry Graham from "Hollywood," Hans Mortier from "Germany," and Gorilla Monsoon from "Parts Unknown." They were aided and abetted by Ralph "Wild Red" Berry.

Dr. Jerry Graham

Jerry Mathews, a.k.a. Dr. Jerry Graham, was a bleached-blonde graduate of the Gorgeous George School of Fashion Design. He was loud, obese, and profane. "The Doctor" was the ultimate heel. He would choke poor Cyclone to within an inch of his life and then claim total innocence when questioned about it. My 8-year-old flame of hope would flicker briefly when Cyclone or Argentino delivered payback. When this happened, Dr. Jerry Graham would fall to his knees, disheveled blonde curls flying everywhere, shaking his head, crossing himself, and begging for mercy. Then the ref would turn his back for half a second, and the suddenly recovered Graham would deliver a low blow to the groin. Finally, in lieu of using a fancy dropkick or a complicated leg-lock, he would end the match by just sitting on the thoroughly beaten Latino. Sadly, this was never enough for The Doctor; even after his hand had been raised in victory, he'd deliver one or two more stomps.

Hans Mortier

His real name was Jacob Grobbe, and he was Dutch, but his character was a hated Nazi, Hans Mortier. Goose-stepping into the ring, he would give a "Sieg Heil" salute, enraging the fans, many of them WWII vets, before the bell even rang. He wore a skullcap, black tights, and jack boots.

Mortier used the same bag of dirty tricks as Dr. Jerry Graham, but with one addition: He would haughtily dare his opponent to hit him in the stomach as hard as possible. The opponent would first look to the crowd for approval (which he naturally received) and then deliver a haymaker straight to the breadbasket. The villainous Mortier would throw back his head and sneer while rippling his stomach muscles like the wave machine at SeaWorld. The desperate opponent might try it again, and sometimes even a third time, but to no avail. Following this little demonstration, Mortier would grab the other wrestlers' face in the dreaded "iron claw." As the clawee writhed in agony, the ref would signal for the bell to ring before the claw hold could, as the announcer warned us, inflict permanent brain damage. The victorious Mortier, accompanied by his gloating manager, would "Sieg Heil" one last blood-boiling time and then goose-step back to the dressing room.

Gorilla Monsoon from "Parts Unknown"

Robert Marella, a.k.a. Gorilla Monsoon, came from that mysterious and forbidden place: "Parts Unknown." I didn't doubt it. He wasn't a wrestler; he was a big, scary, bearded, nonverbal genetic aberration. Again, no flying dropkicks or step-over figure-four leg-locks; he simply hurled Argentino and Cyclone around the ring like soggy chimichangas, communicating his delight in injuring them through a series of grunts and chest-pounding roars. He seemed virtually unbeatable; they would kick him with both feet and even gang up on him, but to no avail. Gorilla Monsoon would simply stampede, smashing them into the turnbuckles again and again, until they collapsed face-down onto the mat. Like Dr. Jerry Graham, he would sit on them, ending their career until the next week.

Since neither Monsoon nor Mortier was particularly skilled in the verbal department, they relied upon the talents of a former wrestler-turned-manager, my first anti-heroic role model, Ralph "Wild Red" Berry.

Wild Red Berry

Wild Red Berry would brazenly enter the ring, sporting a jacket with the words "I Am Right" emblazoned across the back. He carried a small cane, which he used in a variety of situations. He tripped up opponents with it, pointed it at defeated foes, and, of course, jabbed it into the side of Ray Morgan, the unfortunate announcer. During his wrestlers' matches, Berry was a constant thorn in the side of the referee, distracting him while Mortier or Monsoon engaged in their hijinks. He was the antithesis of everything we were raised to believe in. His concept of sportsmanship was to offer a conciliatory handshake to poor Argentino, only to suddenly pull his hand away and simultaneously begin pummeling him with the cane.

While most of the other wrestlers and managers would simply boast of their talents during interviews, Berry would mangle the English language with such rants as: "Let these hams primp their feathers and strut their plumes. I will proceed to maltreat and obliterate them. I will turn loose such terrific voltage and velocity and elliptical trajectory that when it lands on the cleft of the chin it will tear loose their medulla oblongata from the pericardium, cure them of chronic dandruff and knock out four of their impacted wisdom teeth."

Over the years, one of my parents' favorite stories involved their amusement at my obsession with wrestling—and Berry in particular. At one point, it reached such intensity that they thought it worthy of preserving. I was around 10 years old the night they planted a tape recorder under the dinner table. My father proceeded to prompt me with a few questions about wrestling and Wild Red Berry. What followed was part 2 of my "Lord's Prayer" moment: I did my best 10-year-old impression of Wild Red and then provided my own heated commentary regarding his conduct. This would be simply an amusing anecdote except for the fact that my parents played the tape (who knows why?) for a child psychologist. He was horrified and warned them that I was identifying with unhealthy role models. He suggested that I be forbidden to watch wrestling. My parents followed his advice.

I've never known exactly when I first dreamed of being a wrestling manager, but I'm sure that psychologist's warnings about me identifying with grown men from "parts unknown" only intensified my resolve to one day be one of them.

5 DEEP FRIED AND SANCTIFIED, PART 1

Sitting on a couch in Harrisonburg, Virginia, listening to James Brown's *Live at the Apollo* on a summer night in 1978, I sent away for a mail-order minister's license from an ad in the back of Rolling Stone. About two weeks later, I received a certificate and a "love donation" of exactly one cent from First Universal Christian Kingdom. The Rev. Billy C. Wirtz was born.

Rev. Billy Comes to Jesus

Over the next 7 years, my career as a musician/entertainer/one-man freak show began to develop. Harrisonburg was my home base. Like all other small towns, it was both a womb and a trap. It was a place of comfort where I made lifelong friendships that I treasure to this day. It was the place where folks tolerated me at my wildest and my wide-open best and worst. It was the place where I became a fixture (and broke many a fixture) in the local gin mills. It was also the place where, in September 1984, my drinking spun out of control.

Following a drunken blackout and some seriously dangerous behavior committed during a blackout, I realized I needed some help. The next day, I went to see my doctor, who also happened to be a close friend. He sat me down and stared at me for a minute. I realize he was struggling with what he was about to say. Clearing his throat, he actually reached out, took my hand, and in a quiet voice painted a picture that haunts me to this day.

He said, "Billy, you're an alcoholic, and you need to make some decisions.

"Right now?"

"Billy," he said, "you're confused and scared, so let me help you." He continued: "You are a big guy, and you're a nice guy.

31

Nine times out of ten, when you drink, you aren't damaging much besides your wallet and your self-esteem. Unfortunately, that one time that you cross the line, you are capable of some very serious behaviors. If you wish to keep me as your doctor, I am going to offer you two choices. Either you agree to stop drinking and allow random testing for a year, or the next time you come to see me for alcohol-related problems, I will have you committed to Western State for 30 days. I will have them put you in the lockdown ward for terminal alcoholics. You'll be around wet-brained folks who void themselves and scream all night from hallucinations. This is not a threat; this is an ultimatum."

It took me all of about 10 seconds to choose door number one.

The following Monday, I walked into Harrisonburg's lone synagogue, and for the next year and a half, I was an active member of the town's recovery community. A well-known program both saved my life and turned my world upside-down. One of the first things that recovery programs correctly stress is the need to change "playgrounds, playmates and playthings." Unfortunately, the first playmate to go was my girlfriend. My old running buddies didn't turn their backs on me, but it just wasn't the same. I was lonely and restless.

My career was rolling along pretty well. I'd recorded one album, one cassette, and a forty-five of "Stairway to Freebird." At 31 years old, I was working pretty steadily, playing a regional circuit that stretched from Florida to New York. Gradually, thanks to my onstage antics (often appearing in a nurse's outfit and sporting a chainsaw earring), I was building a reputation as an outrageous, unpredictable, always entertaining performer. But a little voice inside me told me it was time to move on. I was a big fish in a little pond, and it was time to jump in the lake.

Movin' On

In the spring of 1986, I played at a dancehall in Hillsboro, North Carolina, opening for my good friends the Nighthawks. I'd finished my set and was signing some autographs when there was a blip on my radar screen.

She was looking for a certain guitarist that she thought might be on the show with us. Fortunately, he'd had to fly to London at the last minute. Seizing the moment, I did my best to convince her that if that certain guitar player had been there, he would have probably unselfishly suggested that she get to know me better. She bought it and gave me her phone number, expecting (as she later confessed) never to hear from me again.

There was something about her that stuck in mind, though, and when I got back home, I called her. After her initial surprise at hearing from me, there were the usual questions: "Are you a real reverend?" "Do you wear nurse's dresses when you're offstage?" "Did you write that really sick song about Marcia Brady?" I passed the quiz, and we got on the topic of pets. At the time, I had two snakes and six tarantulas. Bingo! She turned out to be a reptile enthusiast. Let's see . . . a really attractive, blues-loving, reptile- and arachnid-friendly lady with her own apartment in Raleigh, North Carolina?

We began the series of getting-to-know you hours-long phone calls and decided to meet up in Charleston, South Carolina, for a weekend. There was grumbling about a psycho ex-husband named Charlie. (BTW, ever notice how psycho exes are always named Charlie, Duane, or John Wayne Something?) Other than that, all seemed smooth. It was a great weekend. I played a good gig, and we spent a lot of time discussing reptiles by the pool at the Ramada Inn.

About a month later, she came to visit me in Harrisonburg. Apparently, whatever magic I'd found there escaped her. She described the town as "quaint" and made it clear that she had no interest in spending any time there. So I threw my velvet Elvis paintings, Ric Flair posters, books, snakes, and tarantulas in a much-too-small U-Haul and moved to Raleigh.

About a week before the actual move, we were talking on the phone, and I noticed a not-so-subtle change in her voice. Up until then, every other sentence had begun with "It will be so cool when we . . . " Now it seemed that they all began with "Julia thinks . . . " I figured it might be a little temporary anxiety about suddenly acquiring a roommate she didn't know too well. When she came up to help me move, she gasped in horror at my house cleaning (or lack thereof) skills and informed me not once but several times, "I am a neat freak." I would soon find out how true every word of that declaration was.

It was a disaster from day one. "Don't put your stuff there." "Can you please turn down the TV? I can't sleep." Our intimate moments were often interrupted by phone calls from the drunken ex, who was now threatening physical retaliation. The culmination came one morning, when she woke me up after I'd been asleep for all of three hours: "We need to talk."

In the course of those marathon phone calls, she'd neglected to tell me much about her past. It bordered on unbelievable, but unfortunately, it turned out to be 99% true. Her father was a violent, abusive drunk who'd abandoned her mom shortly after my girlfriend came into the world. Her childhood was one of street-level survival. She grew up in the projects, and she was a survivor—but a deeply scarred one. Apparently, shortly before we met, she had begun seeing a therapist to try and make some sense out of the cards she'd been dealt.

Her therapist, Julia, was a kind, nurturing Asheville free spirit, and my girlfriend worshiped her. Julia convinced her of the need for two important changes.

Change number one: My girlfriend didn't wear make-up, and her wardrobe consisted mainly of band t-shirts and blue jeans. Julia convinced her that she needed to let her femininity blossom. So, she began wearing make-up and buying clothing that didn't hide her rather spectacular figure. This would have been great except for the other important change Julia wanted her to make.

Change number two: Julia also decided that my girlfriend needed to get to know herself without the added burden of being in a committed relationship. It was okay for her to date, even to engage in "casual" sex, but not with someone (me) who had the needs and expectations of a significant other.

Translation: Less than two weeks after leaving all my friends and comfortable surroundings in Virginia, my girlfriend announced that we needed to sleep in separate bedrooms and that she would be "dating" from time to time. Sure enough, within a week, she brought home a guitarist I'd played a few gigs with. He sheepishly waved to me as they disappeared into her bedroom. I spent the rest of the night attempting to find some pliable substance I could fashion into earplugs in order to shut out what sounded like the last two members of an endangered species attempting to ensure their survival on Animal Planet.

Needless to say, the tension became unbearable. And even one dirty dish in the sink was grounds for her to launch into the "I'm a neat freak" lecture. I came within a second of getting drunk in a local bar. I was beginning to get restless.

Movin' On Yet Again

One crisp November morning, the phone rang. A raspy voice inquired, "Is this *the* Reverend Billy C. Wirtz?" I responded with my usual reply: "Does he owe you money?"

He laughed and continued: "This is Bob Greenlee, Root Boy Slim's bass player."

The legendary Root Boy was famous for such tunes as "Boogie Till You Puke" and "Mrs. Paul, Mrs. Paul, Don't You Do Me Like Sarah Lee." I'd worked with him back in 1981, for six insane months, before I went solo full-time. Bob had worked with him before that, and we'd done a series of reunion gigs in the Washington, D.C., area shortly before I'd moved. I guess Bob liked my act because he was calling to offer me a record deal.

Before continuing, I should mention that when you have a unique act like mine, it attracts an array of characters anxious to involve themselves in your career. Over the years, I've been approached by dozens of potential movie directors, would-be agents, management companies, festival organizers and, of course, songwriters (*"Dear Billy, I wrote this one called 'I Drowned Her In MD 20/20 and Married Her Sister!' It's a love song, you can use it if you want!"*).

When Bob proposed a record deal, I was skeptical at first, but when he offered to send me a contract and fly me to Orlando, I began to believe.

A month after I got Bob's call, I found my own little apart-ment in Raleigh, a one-bedroom apartment in the neighborhood bordering North Carolina's maximum-security penitentiary. It wasn't much, but it was a start. I got my first decent night's sleep in three months.

I read the contract that Bob had sent me, thought, "Why not?" and flew to Orlando. As I walked outside the baggage claim area, a white van pulled up. A shirtless black gentleman who intro-duced himself as Louie grabbed my bags and motioned me into the van. Louie was a newcomer to the Orlando area and didn't know the interstates back to the nearby town of Sanford, where Bob operated King Snake Records. We took the main surface road the entire way there. We arrived two hours later, my nerves a bit jangled due to Louie's habit of turning to face me complete-ly while I was talking. We wove in and out of traffic like Jack Webb on nitrous oxide.

By the time we got to King Snake, it was late afternoon, and they were shutting down the studio for the day. Bob checked me into the Sanford Holiday Inn. The hotel was located near a body of water, and no one had bothered to tell me that it was "love bug season" in Florida—or what that meant.

Love bugs are small, harmless insects with very little modesty. They quite happily mate canine style, by the thousands, in mid-air, colliding in mid-stroke with car windshields, sunglasses, and motel room windows. As I sat poolside, enjoying an iced tea, not one but three separate love bug couples utilized my glass as a temporary bridal suite. I couldn't help but laugh as I realized that once again, I was an involuntary bystander witnessing a dance of procreation.

6 DEEP FRIED AND SANCTIFIED, PART 2

I awoke to a beautiful day in Florida. I'd just left rain and general chaos in Raleigh, and it felt more like a vacation than a major career move. Around 10 o'clock, Bob Greenlee came roaring up in his BMW.

Bob looked like anything but a musician and songwriter. He stood 6'3" and weighed in at close to 275 pounds. Indeed, he'd spent his college years on the offensive line at Yale, and he was actually drafted by the Miami Dolphins. He confided in me that after seeing what most football players look like in their 50s, hobbling on broken knees and dealing with residual trauma from head injuries, he opted for another career. Given his wealthy family background, it was expected that he, like his brother, would go into law or a similar profession. But Bob had other plans.

As a teenager, Bob had played with a pair of Daytona natives later known as the Allman Brothers. He had also dared to cross the color line, backing up second-tier black soul acts in the 1960s. In the late 1970s, he'd teamed up with classmate Foster Mackenzie III, a.k.a. Root Boy Slim, and enjoyed fleeting national success unfortunately marred by Slim's mental instability. After a couple years of the nonstop touring circus, Bob left the band and opened King Snake Records.

Take One

That first morning at King Snake, I sat down at the piano and began to go through several of my original compositions. Bob liked about five of them—a good start, but not enough for an album. No problem. He produced a tablet of yellow legal paper, and together we wrote "Beep Tone Blues" and "Your Greens Give Me the Blues." Over the next few days, we managed to lay down the tracks, and the actual recording process went relatively smoothly.

Bob had recently hired an engineer with an extremely impressive national reputation. This guy had played guitar on several multi-platinum albums and knew his way around a studio. Unfortunately, unbeknownst to us, he was going through some difficult times in his personal life that also affected his performance on the job. About a week after we'd finished recording, he handed us the "final" mix. We placed it on the tape machine and listened.

There was my voice, and there was the bass guitar, and way off in the distance there was a cacophony that was, in fact, the other instruments. We were dumbfounded. Maybe something was wrong with the machine.

Just to be safe, Bob called the engineer and asked him to come over right away. We played the tape, and Bob asked, "What's this?" In less than 30 seconds, the engineer went from 0 to 100. His face turned beet red, and a vein in his forehead began to visibly pulsate. He actually began screaming: "It's your f---ing mix, what the f--- do you think it is? Are you f---ing deaf?" He stormed out of the studio, and I never saw him again.

A very subdued Bob drove me back to the motel, where I spent the rest of the day and half the night sitting by the pool, watching love bugs.

Hurry Up and Wait

A year went by before we had a suitable final mix, and then there were problems with the cover art. Another six months went by, three of which I spent in Europe. I came home to a letter from my manager, explaining that he could no longer live on promises and that, effective the first of the year, he was retiring from the music business.

And then, on a cold day in December 1988, the UPS truck pulled up to my little apartment in Raleigh and delivered 25 copies of *Deep Fried and Sanctified*. I played it over and over. Not only did it sound great, but the album cover by Dick Bangum was a twisted work of art.

Getting Noticed

Deep Fried and Sanctified actually made some noise on the national music scene. It got a favorable review in People magazine, a mixed one in Playboy, and "Worst Album of the Year" in Stereo Review. It got airplay on NPR's "Morning Zoo" shows and even a few AM blues stations. One such station in Jacksonville played the 9-minute cut "Roberta" in its warped entirety. As fate would have it, legendary Atlantic Records producer Jerry Wexler happened to be driving through the listening area at the time. He actually stopped and called the station, demanding to know who had sung that song. He said it was the funniest thing he'd heard in years.

My life was about to change again.

Mark Pucci headed up what was probably the best and most honest publicity agency in the business. His contacts ranged from local free music fan papers all the way to Johnny Carson and David Letterman. He pitched *Deep Fried* to several record companies, among them a small label in Oakland, California.

Hightone Records had just struck gold with a good-looking young guitarist named Robert Cray. His last album, *Strong Persuader*, had been optioned by Polygram and gone multi-platinum. It gave Hightone a few dollars with which to sign new artists. After listening to Deep Fried, they decided to take a chance and sign me to a three-record deal.

Back in those days, in order for an album to do any major sales, it was imperative that there be an accompanying video. The folks at Hightone felt that I had the potential to transcend the small blues market niche and become the next Weird Al. They decided to invest in a video, with half the cost to be deducted from future royalties. Of all the songs on the album, the obvious candidate for the video was a song I'd written back in the early 1980s. It paid homage to a female midget wrestler I remembered from my youth, named Diamond Lil. The song was titled "Teenie Weenie Meanie."

OCCUPATION: RED HEADED GEEK

7 "TEENIE WEENIE MEANIE"

The record company had decided that "Teenie Weenie Meanie" had the best chance of pleasing the folks at MTV. I was thrilled. There was only one slight logistical glitch: Where and how would we find my leading lady?

Fortunately, Raleigh, North Carolina, was one of the major hubs of the National Wrestling Alliance. Dorton Arena still hosted wrestling once a month, and it ran shows the old-fashioned way: "Want a beer? How about six?" "Smoking section, you're sittin' in it." There was the toothless senior citizen with the sign pinned to his shirt announcing, "I do not hear, please help me to make a living," selling programs and pencils, just as he had for the past 40 years. There was even a VIP section for season ticket holders. The ringside seats were reserved, but if you missed more than two cards in a row, they sold your seat. I went to several cards there and never saw those seats change hands; as a matter of fact, the wrestlers recognized most of the regulars and quite frequently played off of them during the matches.

The local wrestling promoter also ran one of the nightspots in town where I played, so he was my obvious first pick for finding my costar. When I told him I needed a midget lady wrestler, he neither batted an eye nor hesitated. He got out a pen and a sticky note and wrote down the name Lillian Ellison, with a South Carolina number.

Finding My Leading Lady

I called the South Carolina number, and a woman answered.

"May I speak with Lillian?"

"Speaking."

"Hi, Lillian. My name is Reverend Billy C. Wirtz, and I'm a musician. I've written a song about a guy in love with a midget wrestler, and my record company wants me to do a video of it. The booker in Raleigh told me you might be able to help."

(Pause) "Reverend who?"

"Rever—"

"You're a preacher?'

"Well, not exactly, I'm a musician and a major wrestling fan, and—"

"You're a wrestling fan?"

"Yes, ma'am. Are you?"

"I guess so. I've been a wrestler for 50 damn years!"

"I'm sorry, ma'am, I've never heard—"

"Does The Fabulous Moolah ring a bell?"

"Oh my Lord, yes!!"

"You're talking to her."

It took me a minute to regain my composure. The Fabulous Moolah was *the* queen of women's wrestling. She began her career in the 1950s, and in 1989, she was still active in the ring, having been a major part of the original WrestleMania, going up against Cowgirl Wendi Richter and Cindy Lauper in the match that launched the marriage of rock 'n' roll and wrestling.

I apologized profusely, but she cut me off: "You need a damn midget?"

I told her that indeed I did, the song was based on a childhood crush I had on a wrestler named Diamond Lil.

Moolah laughed: "She's standing right here."

I stared at the phone in disbelief.

"Are you—?"

"Am I what?

"Are you bullsh---ing me?"

"You want to speak to her?"

"Katie, come here and say hi to this man."

A soft voice simply said, "Hi."

It turned out that Lil's real name was Katie. Again, I was tongue-tied, but before I could respond, Moolah had regained possession of the phone. "You want to use her in a video? Where are you going to shoot it, and how much are you payin' her?"

"We're going to shoot it in Raleigh, I'll need her for one day, and we can pay her $500."

(Pause) "That's not very much. What kind of a song is it?" This isn't a bunch of that rap sh-t, is it?" (Moolah had quite the vocabulary for a senior citizen.)

I told her it was a fun song and that I could overnight a copy to her. That seemed to suit her fine. I hung up the phone and set a land-speed record getting to the post office in time to send out a copy of the album.

Two days later, Lillian called me back: "Five hundred bucks, a motel room, and gas money."

"Deal."

Meeting Moolah and Katie

The record company made the arrangements with an LA-based producer, wired $500 to my bank account, and told me to be ready to go the following Monday at 6 a.m.

Moolah and Katie arrived Sunday night. At about 7 that evening, I got a call. A sugar-sweet voice said, "Hey, baby, I'm at the motel, waitin' on you!" This was followed by a raucous laugh, and Moolah gently suggesting, "Get your ass up here, and bring the money."

I knocked on the door, and there she was: the queen of the squared circle: blonde hair, a beige form-fitting sweater, matching slacks, and, around her neck, a diamond-encrusted solid-gold dollar sign. She could have been a once-famous movie starlet; even at her age, she radiated confidence and an awareness of who she was. She was damn fine looking. The only visible sign of her occupation was a nose that had obviously been broken too many times to bother resetting.

She looked me up and down and then, smiling like we'd known each other all our lives, invited me in and pointed to her companion sitting by the bed.

"Katie, this is Billy. Billy, this is Katie, my damn midget." She noticed my shock at the introduction and laughed. "Don't worry," she said, "that's just what I call her, I love her more than anyone in the world."

We chatted for a while. She told me she loved the song, thought it was real cute. Anything I wanted Katie to do, I was to tell Moolah, and she would decide if it was okay. I quickly realized that political incorrectness aside, Moolah was fiercely protective of Katie and served as her buffer to the outside world. We ran over the basic shooting script, and I excused myself, feeling inexplicably tired all of a sudden.

By 5:30 the next morning, every part of my body hurt. My legs burned, my arms felt like they weighed 200 pounds, it hurt to even blink my eyes. I had a hellfire case of the flu. I took my temperature. 101.5. I called my manager and croaked out the bad news, begging him to postpone the shoot. Unfortunately, our budget was stretched right down to the last penny, and there was no wiggle room. The record company was already in the hole to the tune of around 20 grand.

I called Moolah, and the queen of women's wrestling suddenly became Florence Nightingale. "Oh, sugar, I am so sorry. You're gonna be okay, Katie's all ready, and I'll take care of you, and I won't let them push you too hard." Between the flu and her comforting voice, I was on the verge of tears. I thanked her and told her I'd see her in an hour.

The Shoot: Los Angeles Meets Irmo, South Carolina

We shot the video at three locations:

• *The Brewery, a well-known bar in Raleigh*—We converted the stage into a makeshift-wrestling ring.

• *The parking lot of CC's, a local gay bar*—The club patrons' orientation had nothing to do with the video; the place just had a parking lot with a stage entrance.

• *A mobile home dealership*—We needed a doublewide to shoot the scenes of domestic bliss.

We started at the Brewery. When we arrived, they'd already set up the lights and the ring. The first shot involved me watching Katie in a wrestling match. Moolah would be her opponent. She instructed Katie to put her in a headlock and then take her to the floor with a leg sweep.

The nervous young LA director apparently had been absent from class the day they taught how to work with pro "rasslers" in film school. He called, "Action!" Katie grabbed Moolah and put her in the headlock. Moolah let out a bloodcurdling "AAAAAH," selling the move the best she could. She gave Katie the signal, and with a crash that echoed off the walls, Moolah executed a perfect fall.

"OH MY GOD!!" the director screamed, ripping off his headset and running to the stage. "Cut, cut, cut." He was waving his arms, about to have an aneurysm. "Are you okay? Do you need a doctor?" he frantically asked Moolah.

With a look of total disdain, she looked at him and said, "What the f--- is your problem?"

The assembled cast, crew, and extras, me included, tried not to roll on the floor with hysterical laughter at this meeting of the Los Angeles and Irmo, South Carolina, schools of acting. After assuring him that she was fine, Moolah politely inquired, "Do you want another take?"

The rest of day went relatively smoothly, and as we set up for other shots, Moolah told me about how she and Katie had met up. What follows is her account of their meeting; I've never forgotten it.

"You Just Can't Find Good Midgets Anymore"

Back in the 1960s, the various wrestling federations had weekly circuits. A typical week might look like this:

Monday—Charlotte, North Carolina

Tuesday—Greensboro, North Carolina

Wednesday—Columbia, South Carolina

Thursday—Travel

Friday—Richmond, Virginia

Saturday afternoon—Watch TV

Saturday night—Winston-Salem, North Carolina

Sunday afternoon—Hickory, North Carolina

The average wrestler traveled over 100,000 miles a year, doing over 300 one-nighters.

Moolah had a big following in several cities, and one of her best was Richmond. Back in the early 1960s, she began noticing a certain girl showing up at all her matches. In those days, fans could approach the wrestlers in the ring before the match and get autographs. This particular girl, Katie, had asked Moolah for hers several times. Moolah couldn't help but notice that this woman was a little person. One night Moolah also noticed that the girl had a black eye. Moolah asked what had happened, and the girl answered, "Oh, I tripped over the dog." A couple weeks later, once again, the girl had a black eye, with some swelling underneath it. When Moolah questioned her, Katie mumbled a reply but didn't make eye contact. Moolah told her: "Stick around after the matches. I want to talk to you."

Katie stuck around, and after the matches, they went back to the dressing room. "Okay, what happened?"

"Nothing, I just—"

"Don't lie to me. What happened?"

"My daddy drinks, and sometimes—"

"He's not going to ever do that again. Go get your jacket; you're coming home with me."

Moolah shook her head as she recounted the scene to me. "Billy, I taught her how to read and write. She was 17 and couldn't really do either." She let that sink in and then explained, "I had to get her a job, and no one wanted to hire her, so I taught her how to wrestle. At the time, there were men midgets, but no girl midget wrestlers. Billy, we made a killing, especially over in Asia, places like Malaysia and Singapore. Damn, they loved those midget girls. Hell, I bet I had 15 of them workin' for me at one time." Shakings her head in disbelief, she said, "You just can't find good midgets anymore."

Video Debut

The "Teenie Weenie Meanie" video was shot in a day and released within a week. We sent it to MTV, and they passed on it. VH1 passed, too. However, the folks at USA Networks' *Up All*

Night loved it and scheduled it to run the following Saturday at the stroke of midnight.

The following Saturday, I was playing at The Decade in Pittsburgh. I was opening for a local hero, Norm Nardini. Halfway through my set, I noticed a commotion by the back door. Two enormous humans marched in, and as they stepped aside, in walked Jon Bon Jovi. The place went nuts. I've had a few brushes with really famous people over the years, and Bon Jovi was probably the nicest of them all. He laughed at my song about surfing Mennonites and asked me to send him a copy of my new album, leaving me his personal mailbox address. Next thing I knew, it was 11:50.

What a break! My video was about to debut on national TV, and Bon Jovi was in the house. I began to prepare my Grammy acceptance speech. I held my breath and heard the host of the show announce my video: "And here it is, the new one by Rev. Bobby Werth." Two minutes into it, they cut away to an Old Spice commercial. Bon Jovi smiled, patted me on the shoulder, said "Bummer," and then quickly exited out the back door.

"It Helps to Know Somebody"

About a month after the "Teenie Weenie Meanie" video first aired, I noticed a New Jersey exchange on my answering machine. Years ago, while playing with my first road band, I'd met a trumpet player from New Jersey named Tony Pallagrosi. He was right out of central casting, with moussed hair and designer jeans that outlined every portion of his Italian manhood. When challenged or threatened, his standard response was, "Hey, he's nobody. One phone call, and he's history. I know people."

Beneath it all, Tony was a really sweet guy. By the time "Teenie Weenie Meanie" was released, Tony had long since gotten out of the playing side of the business and gone into promoting shows. When he said he knew people, at least in the state of New

Jersey, he pretty much did. Among his friends was a former club bouncer turned pro wrestler named Page Falkenberg, known professionally as Diamond Dallas Page.

Tony had called me about a gig in Asbury Park, and during the conversation, I told him about the new album, the video, and my brush with Bon Jovi (another friend of his). Tony offered his sympathy about the video debut and as a gesture of friendship offered to send a copy of the video to Page. Tony explained, "He might know somebody who knows somebody."

Two weeks later, I had another call on my machine: "Hey, Rev. It's DDP, Diamond Dallas Page. Love that video, brother. Listen, I'm doing color commentary for Florida wrestling. We've been talking about adding some music in between the matches and were wondering if you'd like to make a guest appearance."

The show went great. We shot it before a live audience in Tampa. Also on the show was a great local band, the Johnny G. Lyon band. They knew "Teenie Weenie Meanie," so we played it, and during the guitar solo, I went berserk. I gave the piano a Dusty Rhodes bionic elbow smash, I put the claw hold on the bass player . . . it was a riot. At the end of the song, Dallas called me over to his desk. At the time, the PTL scandal was all over the news, and Dallas asked me what I thought of Jim Bakker. I responded with something like: "You know, Dallas, there are real men, and there are near-men; there are originators, and there are imitators. Jim Bakker is an example of what happens when they cross-breed humans with planarian worms, and if Tammy Faye ever spent an hour with me, I'd give her a good reason to scream 'Hallelujah!'"

They cut to a commercial. Dallas looked at me and said, "Hey, Rev, you're a natural."

Mike Graham, one of the producers, came out and was likewise complimentary. I knew it was now or never. I thanked them both, and asked, "So, how do you get to be one of the managers?"

Mike responded: "Well, it helps to know somebody. It's even better if you look pretty wild (like 6′4″ with flame-red hair and chainsaw earrings?). And you need to be able to be able to work the mic and get people all riled up."

I didn't say anything. He thought for a minute and said the words I'd been waiting almost 30 years to hear: "Why don't you give me a call tomorrow?"

8 TRADITIONS AND THE WRESTLING BUSINESS

Before I continue with my story, I want to let you in on some things I learned in my first couple weeks as a wrestling manager. I should also remind you that this is not a "wrestling book" any more than *Ball Four* was a book about major league baseball. Almost any other book about wrestling will tell you about behaviors and politics I knew nothing about and/or never witnessed. I don't doubt they happened, but I went out of my way to avoid certain situations.

I really liked working for the PWF: The folks there treated me great and with respect. The WCW was a little different. I couldn't believe that a multi-million-dollar business could be so disorganized. They never treated me or the band badly; it was just perpetual chaos. One floor director would tell us one thing, and five minutes later, someone else would tell us something completely different. On the couple of occasions when I questioned the reasoning behind some last-minute script or programming change, the standard response was "It's wrestling."

Getting into the Wrestling Business 20 Years Ago

In the 1990s, professional wrestling was the ultimate example of a closed shop. Of all the areas of show business I've been involved with, it was by far and without a doubt the trickiest and hardest to break into, even as a supporting character. On the other hand, I found out that for the actual wrestlers, the necessary steps were pretty well defined.

The process of becoming a pro wrestler was simple, at least on paper. There were a couple dozen wrestling schools that a young man (or woman) of sound mind and body could apply to.

The basic training ran around $3,000 and lasted anywhere from 6 to 10 weeks. Some of the schools made Marine boot camp look like a walk in the park. On the very first day, the new students were pushed past their limit doing exercises alone. If the students passed that, then they were taught the basics: how to fall, how to perform certain basic moves, and how to "work" a match. A wrestling match is far more than a couple of guys throwing each other around for a few minutes. It is truly a mini-soap opera (or, as we call it, rope opera), complete with near-falls, breathtaking high-risk spots, and, often, surprise endings that continue the story line.

Much like in any other area of entertainment, in wrestling, there are certain individuals who have the X factor: that indefinable charisma, either good or bad, that sets them apart from the pack. Very often the instructors in the schools will notice them and bring them to the attention of booking agents in the pro ranks. It usually takes a couple years to develop a character and to sell him to the general public, but every now and then, a wrestler will go from 0 to 100 in a matter of weeks.

Several WCW wrestlers discovered Bill Goldberg when he was working as a bouncer in an Atlanta strip club. A former football player for University of Georgia and briefly for the Atlanta Falcons (where he had a reputation as being a bit of a loose cannon), Goldberg was incredibly strong. During one of his early matches in Washington, D.C., the fans began to chant "Goldberg, Goldberg, Goldberg." A certain soundman recorded the chant and put it on a loop. Within a month, every time he appeared, they would play the chant over the P.A., and the fans in the house would begin to follow along.

During the time I worked with the WCW, the walls of the MGM Grand in Las Vegas would literally shake with the sound of "Goldberg, Goldberg, Goldberg," in anticipation of his arrival. In fact, he was still really "green," and so it was up to the more experienced wrestlers to "put him over"—that is, make him look good. Some of the others who'd been there for years and hadn't moved up the ranks as fast as Goldberg had resented him, but for the most part, they were willing to put him over, knowing that not doing so could negatively impact their own careers.

Behind the Curtain

Wrestling has always existed in its own very tightly knit world. Even in the late 1980s, many of the old carny traditions still existed. I'll describe some of them here.

Kayfabe

Kayfabe (pronounced "kay-fabe") is the portrayal of events in wrestling as unstaged. It's also the freeze-out employed when there are outsiders present. In the wrestling world, you're either "one of the boys" and "smart," or you're not. If an outsider questions one about the business, there's no such thing as lying. Any explanation, no matter how ludicrous or blatantly untrue, is acceptable. In short, we protect our own. When an outsider is present, a "smart" individual will drop *kayfabe* into the conversation ("Hey, Billy, did you play a gig last night at the Kayfabe Lounge?").

Secret Signs and Language

There is indeed a secret handshake among wrestlers. And they use a form of pig-Latin known as Ceezarny. Ceezarny involves placing the letters *eez* behind the first letter of a word. For example, in Ceezarny, Billy is "Beezilly," carny is "ceezarny," and business is "beezisiness." Wrestlers use it in the ring when whispering directions to each other, and also in day-to-day conversation.

The Code of Conduct

The number-one, nonnegotiable rule of professional wrestling is that you never intentionally hurt another wrestler. He has a family to feed, and if he is injured, they may not eat. This is the foundation on which all other rules of the business are based.

On occasion, either out of carelessness, vanity, or stupidity, someone violates this rule. When that occurs, the punishment is swift and severe. Often the violator is someone new to the business; maybe they've gotten little carried away with being on TV, and they begin to think that the rules don't apply to them. After they have committed the infraction, often their next match is with "a hooker." A hooker in the wrestling world is an older wrestler, often someone who is in the twilight of their career. What the hooker may lack in youth he or she makes up in strength and meanness. Quite often, the hooker will intentionally break a finger, a toe, or even an arm or a leg. I've seen more than one flashy young upstart scream in real pain as a little finger is broken by an old-timer. Fortunately, most newcomers are entering the business a lot "smarter" than in previous years, and the need for hookers has dramatically decreased.

"Stooge-ing"

This does not mean going around doing Curly impressions. Rather, it's a term used to describe telling (and selling) the secrets of the business to outsiders. Next to intentionally hurting another wrestler, stooge-ing the business is considered the second most serious transgression. Over the years, a certain amount of stooge-ing has always occurred. In the late 1950s, Wild Red Berry admitted to Groucho Marx that the outcomes of the matches were often predetermined. He did stress, however, that the numerous injuries that wrestlers live with are very real.

One of the most famous stooge-ing incidents occurred in 1983, when a mid-carder by the name of Eddie Mansfield did a tell-all interview with John Stossel on *20/20*. He not only told Stossel that the moves were choreographed, he explained the practice of "blading," described next.

Blading

At one time, there was a saying "Red brings green," meaning that the bloodier the matches, the better. Indeed, wrestling magazines often featured covers of men whose faces were, in the words of legendary announcer Gordon Solie, "a crimson mask." There was much speculation as to how the blood was drawn. I've heard everything from blood capsules, to chicken blood, to ketchup. The truth is a bit more grisly: In the business, it's known as blading, and wrestlers who agree to blade receive a pay bump.

In blading, a wrestler takes an old-style double-edged razor blade and cuts off a tiny portion of the blade, about the size of this: ^. He then wraps it in adhesive tape around his forefinger. At a given signal in the match, he rolls out of sight of the audience and the camera, (lightly) jabs himself in the forehead, and gives a slight tug. The resulting wound is (hopefully) not too deep; the thinness of the skin combined with sweat often makes it appear far worse than it is.

The fans go crazy.

Find some pictures of older wrestlers and look at their foreheads. You'll notice that many of them look like a roadmap of Miami. The old-school guys wear their blading scars with pride, much like cauliflower ears. Blading, though still done occasionally, has fallen out of favor, as Vince McMahon and company have tried to "clean up" wrestling's image. Also, the spread of AIDS in the 1980s made the practice much less popular.

(Remember that Moolah warned me, "Just don't let 'em blade you, Sugar"? This is what she was talking about.)

Mansfield's Stooge-ing: What Happened Next

After Mansfield had explained blading in graphic detail, Stossel took it upon himself to confront another wrestler to verify some of Mansfield's allegations. He managed to make it to the door of the dressing room at a WWF show. At first, Vince

McMahon was cooperative, but upon realizing what was up, he kayfabed Stossel. What happened next has been the subject of much speculation over the years, but basically, Stossel confronted Dave "Dr. Death" Schultz outside the dressing room. Over the years, many have said that Schultz was acting under orders to "take him out." Regardless, when Stossel asked him point-blank "Is it fake?" Schultz responded with an open-hand slap that sent Stossel sprawling and taunted him with the words, "Is that fake? Does that feel fake, boy?"

When they cut back to the studio, Stossel's co-hosts expressed horror and indignation at such a barbaric act. Stossel reported that he had been to see his doctor, been x-rayed for a possible head injury, and was considering legal action.

The final result was typical of the wrestling business. Rather than have sympathy for Stossel, most wrestling fans agreed that he had it coming and he was lucky to have gotten off that easy.

McMahon made no comment, except to note that his box office receipts actually increased as a result. Shortly thereafter, Dave Schultz retired from the ring and opened a private detective agency, and within a couple months, Mansfield was again booking shows in Florida.

It's wrestling.

Then and Now: Changes in the World of Wrestling

As best I can remember, Mansfield was the first to go public and break kayfabe. Since then, the practice has become an industry in itself. Numerous documentaries and dozens of first-person accounts graphically describe truly shocking and egregious behavior. The Internet is loaded with "insider" sites.

The price of fame has escalated tenfold from what it was when I was in the business. The immortal (that's how they used to refer to him anyway) Hulk Hogan probably has nights he wishes he were back working at the bar in Florida where he was once the doorman. Ever since his reality show tanked, his life has been a series of continuous public humiliations. As of last week, he had been reduced to pimping rental furniture.

In wrestling today, even the staging is staged. Modern technology makes it possible to make half-empty arenas appear to be packed to the rafters. Entrance themes get more reaction than the matches themselves. "Valets" have replaced managers, and wrestlers read scripted interviews off tele-prompters. In the world of WWE doublespeak, the term *wrestling*, the very name of the business itself, has been replaced by the far less threatening moniker "sports entertainment."

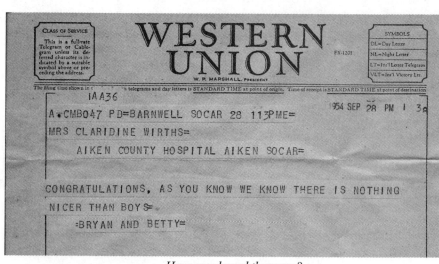

CLASS OF SERVICE

This is a full-rate Telegram or Cablegram unless its deferred character is indicated by a suitable symbol above or preceding the address.

WESTERN UNION

W. P. MARSHALL, PRESIDENT

FX-1201

SYMBOLS

DL=Day Letter
NL=Night Letter
LT=Int'l Letter Telegram
VLT=Int'l Victory Ltr.

The filing time shown in t ʼn telegrams and day letters is STANDARD TIME at point of origin. Time of receipt is STANDARD TIME at point of destination

IA A36

A▪CMB047 PD=BARNWELL SOCAR 28 113PME=

1954 SEP 28 PM I 3₉

MRS CLARIDINE WIRTHS=

AIKEN COUNTY HOSPITAL AIKEN SOCAR=

CONGRATULATIONS, AS YOU KNOW WE KNOW THERE IS NOTHING
NICER THAN BOYS=
=BRYAN AND BETTY=

Have you heard the news?

Left- 1960-My first publicity photo (taken around the time of "The Lord's Prayer" performance).

Below- The Wirths family-Christmas, 1997. Left to Right- . Ted , David, Claudine, me and Sheeba.

1958- One of my early character parts, age 4.

1957-The infamous "Zorro" costume. I woke my mom up for three straight nights needing assurance that Santa Claus knew just what I wanted.

1967-The future Rock 'N" Roll singer. Before piano, there was the guitar.

1972-High School graduation.

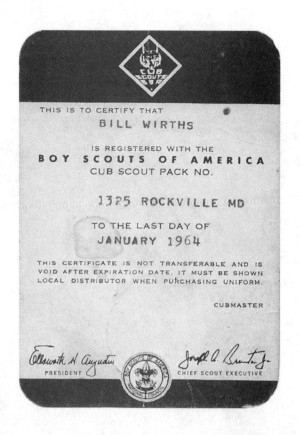

Pack 1325 Cub Scouts Rockville, Md.

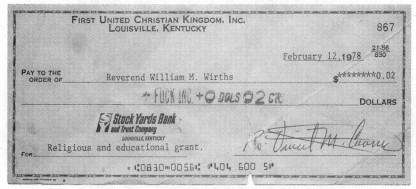

My first "love" offering. Notice the name of the Church.

Publicity photo 1982 "Salvation Thru Polyester."

Dough-re-mi (one of my numerous live bits).

*Above- "Teenie Weanie Meanie" with the John-
nie G. Lyons Band.*

Below- Applying a headlock to myself.

My first appearance as a manager- with Coach
John Heath and D.D.P.

Rev. Billy and the Disciples. (Jumbo Baretta and
Dennis Knight).

A brief moment of quiet reflection (left) just before inciting the
masses (right).

"Talkin" that talk." The Coach, me , Jumbo
Baretta and Dallas Page.

"We have the belts!" Me, Coach, Dallas and the Bounty
Hunters (Al Green-L, Tim "Powerhouse" Parker-R).

WCW MONDAY NITRO "Nitecap."

9 WELCOME TO THE PWF

Following Mike Graham's invitation to give him a call, I must have gone through three phone cards, dialing friends and family from the luxurious Red Roof Inn in Tampa.

The first night I stayed there, while enjoying a late-night snack at the Village Inn next door, I got into a conversation with a couple members of the Hillsborough County Sheriff's Department. When the conversation got around to what I was doing in town, I told them that I had just signed on with the PWF. I was about to explain what the initials represent, but that was unnecessary; one of the deputies held up his hand, saying: "We know all too well what that stands for. Be careful with that bunch."

The deputy started naming most of the wrestlers I would be working with, recounting their not-so-occasional brushes with local law enforcement. The deputies then began to talk about some wrestlers of past years, and gradually I got the feeling that the Sheriff's Department saw them as sort of overgrown juvenile delinquents rather than hardened criminals. With that reassurance, I finished my club sandwich and turned in for the night.

The next day, I met Mike Graham and Steve Keirn at the television studios, where they filled me in on who I'd be working with. We hadn't been talking for more than 15 minutes when a phone call came in. Apparently, one of our wrestlers had gotten "The Call."

In pro wrestling, "The Call" meant that one of the two major companies—the World Wrestling Federation (referred to as New York) or World Championship Wrestling (referred to as Atlanta)—had called a particular wrestler for a try-out. This was the equivalent of being called up from the minor leagues to the majors. One of the unspoken rules of the wrestling business is that situations, careers, and opportunities usually present themselves on a moments' notice. If someone received "The Call," it was perfectly understandable, even encouraged, that they act on it immediately. Even if it necessitated changing the script of the entire show, no one held taking "The Call" against a wrestler because it meant a shot at the big time.

The Show Must Go On

So there we were, with an hour to go before show time, and the current belt-holder of the Florida title was on his way to Atlanta. When it comes to last-minute changes in the program and the ability to go with the flow, nothing compares to professional wrestling. Quite often, I saw an entire story line reconstructed during the Abdominizer commercial preceding the next scheduled match. At least half the time, I would be given approximately 10 minutes to come up with a reason a certain wrestler would not be showing up, even though we'd been running promos for a week beforehand, promising his appearance.

The announcer (usually Dallas) would say something like, "Wrestling fans, I've just received word that we have a last-minute change in the program. Maybe Mike Graham or someone in charge can explain." Instead, I would come strutting out, much to the chagrin of the fans and the announcers alike.

After grabbing the microphone away from Dallas in midsentence, I'd start in with something like: "Well, it's a pleasure to be here with all of my fans!" (loud boos from the crowd) " . . . and of course, the usual genetic misfits they let in this place" (louder boos). "Dallas, I'm sorry to break the news to you, but it looks like (certain wrestler) was so scared of having to face one of Rev. Billy's Flock that he hitched his doublewide to the back of the short school bus that he travels in and headed back to his job as a quality control inspector at the sper . . . I mean poultry plant." (pause and let the heckling build) "I'll tell you what. Since the title is technically vacant, much like the cranial areas of most of our studio audience . . . " (really loud boos) "EXCUSE ME!! Would you people kindly shut up while I'm trying to talk?" (crowd starts chanting "Red Headed Geek, Red Headed Geek!" I look at them in disgust) "This Saturday night, we'll have a tournament for the vacant title. That's assuming that any of these other Hefty bags with a pulse that you call wrestlers are man enough to step in the ring with one of the Flock. Does that sound okay to you?"

Dallas starts to say something, but before he can speak, I grab the mic: "I thought that's what you'd say." I throw down the microphone and walk off, the crowd still taunting me: "Red Headed Geek, Red Headed Geek!!"

(Damn, that was fun.)

Career Choices: Music , Comedy, or Wrestling?

I wondered if I could successfully transition from music and stand-up comedy to wrestling.

In comedy and music, you do your best to win over the crowd and get them to like you. The exact opposite is true in wrestling: As a manager, it's your duty to irritate the piss out of them any way you can. You're expected to be rude, annoying, conceited, a nonstop motor-mouth, and, when confronted by the "baby-face," a total coward. I loved it. After a night of getting paid for engaging in a convoluted form of primal scream therapy, I was as peaceful and calm as if I'd just eaten bar-b-que with the Dalai Lama.

A little inside secret: As a manager, your main function is to "put over" the "baby-face," or good guy. I often used personal insults, making fun of his clothing or grooming—the meaner the better. Wrestling uses TV to promote live, or "house," shows. Frequently, I would start a feud on TV, to be resolved at the live show. Hopefully, I was either obnoxious enough or funny enough to draw in fans intent on seeing me shut up.

There are some similarities between wrestling, comedy, and music. However, there's one major difference, which ultimately helped me to make some difficult career choices: Both music and comedy have numerous levels at which one can work and make a decent living. In both comedy and music, even if the big break never happens, it's still possible to make a good living up to and even past retirement age.

A good musician, even if he or she never becomes a household name, can put bread on the table playing locally, giving lessons, doing studio work, and any number of other ways. In any given metro area, there are probably 100 full-time musicians who never leave the city limits and are able to make a decent living.

Comics all aspire to national television. Needless to say, the odds of that happening are astronomical, and few succeed at getting that far. However, a good comic can also make a decent paycheck with no TV exposure. Comics can work as the resident emcee in metropolitan comedy clubs, on the road on the bar circuit, on cruise ships, in casinos, and even (especially here in Florida) in retirement homes. Once again, there's enough work to pay the bills.

In wrestling, there are two levels: big time and small time. And then there are a couple other options as well: the fair circuit and Japan.

The Big Time

The big time in wrestling means one thing: WWE. There are a couple other national outfits, but even they rely heavily on former WWE talent. Although Titan Sports (the WWE parent company) is located in Connecticut, the wrestlers refer to it as New York. I don't know exactly what the starting wrestlers make, and for that matter, neither do they. Basically, it's whatever Titan Sports sends you in your paycheck. I think it often starts with a few hundred dollars per match. Depending on several factors, a superstar like The Rock or Steve Austin can make millions—and then there are endorsements, sales of action figures, and action films.

There is a catch, though: The WWE owns the copyright on your character. Many a foolish wrestler has walked out thinking he has sufficient name recognition to go it on his own. The lucky ones usually end up on C-list reality shows.

The Small Time

The small time is where you start out and where you end up after you've (hopefully) spent some time in the big leagues. It's made up of local independent promotions, some of them with weekly TV tapings. Standard pay is usually gas money plus $50, or on a big show $100, but that's rare.

The Fair Circuit

There's actually something of an interim level on the independent scene, known as the fair circuit. Independent promoters run these shows. A typical card might open with a couple local wrestlers looking for exposure, then feature a mid-card match usually with a couple of "legends," and wrap up with a headline match with at least one bona fide "star." Very often, the "star" will be someone who has been on TV in the past year.

The fair circuit is a rough way to make a buck for all parties concerned. Quite often, the promoter will contact a wrestler, and the wrestler will demand a 50% deposit, a plane ticket, and whatever else can be negotiated. The promoters hope the wrestlers will show up, and the wrestlers hope the promoters don't skip out. The ring itself can be an adventure—sometimes secure, sometimes not. The mats can be clean and disinfected or dilapidated and bloodstained. There is one plus: The wrestlers can often offset their expenses and beef up their pay by selling t-shirts and charging $5 apiece for autographs. It's far from glamorous, but it beats not working—if only barely.

Japan

There's one last option for wrestlers, and many of them do opt for this, though, unfortunately, managers are not generally part of the script. Even though there are some initial language barriers, there's a good living to be made in Japan.

Beginning in the late 1940s, American wrestlers began going to Japan to work as "heels" (bad guys).For a country that had been devastated by a war, pro wrestling offered the Japanese their first opportunity to see their countrymen (and women) defeating the "round eyes." To this day, wrestling is still tremendously popular there. I've had numerous wrestlers tell me that the pay is fabulous, but the Japanese like to see lots of blood, and they work extremely "stiff."

Survey Says . . . Wrestling

Whatever skills I brought over from music and comedy seemed to work in establishing my place in the wrestling business. I hadn't been there more than a month when I heard that I was being "watched" by the big league scouts. Although I left too soon to find out if that was true, I did get a taste of the big time down the road.

Meanwhile, back in Tampa . . .

Webster's defines *mania* as "Excitement manifested by mental and physical hyperactivity, disorganization of behavior, and elevation of mood."

One of the noticeable differences separating pro wrestling from other forms of entertainment is the constant manic energy level at which it operates. TV tapings reminded me of a chase scene on *Benny Hill*.

From the opening segment to the final credits, everything is in a constant state of flux, and whether it's the PWF or the WCW, everyone is constantly running around, wondering what the flux is going on. To give you an idea of what I mean, let's look at a typical TV show.

The Shooting Script

Here's what a show's shooting script might look like, in all its gory detail:

14:00–14:10—Opening sequence, roll clip from the end of last week's show, Magnificent Mephisto challenges the All-American Kid to a haircut match

14:10–14:12—Abdominizer commercial

14:12–14:20—First match: Hollywood Ned vs. Farmer Roy

14:20–14:23—Juice-O-Matic commercial

14:23–14:33—Second match: Bounty Hunter #2 vs. The Masked E.M.T., followed by interview with Rev. Billy after match

14:33–14:35—Upcoming shows bumper

14:35–14:40—Interview with Big Daddy Don, roll clip from last week's house show. Reverend interrupts interview to challenge Big Daddy. Bounty Hunter #2 run-in.

14:40–14:42—Abdominizer commercial

14:42–14:44—Big Daddy challenges Bounty Hunters to a two-on-one match this Saturday night at Eddie Graham Center; if Big Daddy wins, he gets 30 seconds in the ring with Rev. Billy.

14:44–14:45—Juice-O-Matic commercial

14:46–14:56—Florida Championship match. Exterminator vs. Seminole Kid. Bounty Hunter #1 does run-in, Big Daddy does run-in. D.Q. with ref-bump

14:56–14:57—Upcoming show promo

14:57–15:00—Replay last minutes of final match, voiceover from announcer, roll credits.

Reality Check

Now that you've seen the script for a show, here's what really goes on:

45 minutes before showtime—The Magnificent Mephisto has not shown up yet. After a series of frantic phone calls, the producer tells us that Mephisto got pulled over, his license is expired, but the cop recognized him and let him go with a warning. Someone will need to pay his cab fare when he gets here.

30 minutes before showtime—Farmer Roy calls from the airport, saying he's just gotten "The Call." He's been trying to get through to the TV station for the last half-hour, but the line has been busy. So now Hollywood Ned will go up against The Jokerman, a former employee who flunked his last drug test and is looking to get his old job back so just happens to be

backstage. The Jokerman agrees to wrestle, on the condition that he gets rehired for at least another four shows so he can pay his back child support.

10 minutes before showtime—The Big Daddy Don spot is to be switched with the Bounty Hunter interview, for no apparent reason.

1 minute before showtime—Exterminator and the producer are in a back room, shouting at each other. We hear something being thrown, the door opens, and all is settled.

Who's Backstage

You'll notice several different groups of people backstage. Most of them fall into one of the following categories.

The Talent

The talent consists of the wrestlers and characters around whom the show is built. They usually fall into one of three sub-categories:

1. *Wrestlers who are part of the regular series*—These are usually young up-and-comers who show promise and are looking to move up to the majors.

2. *Established "name" wrestlers who are contracted to do a series of shows*—Often these are older wrestlers in the twilight of their careers who still have drawing power. They are treated with the respect shown to nobility in any profession. In some cases, they can be prima donnas. Most of the time, however, they offer encouragement and advice to young, inexperienced manager types, and they often reappear later on in one's career, putting in the word with key people in bigger organizations.

3. *Managers, valets, and referees*—These are the folks who play supporting roles. We often sit back and listen to the wres-

tlers and talk with each other—about the business, whose star is rising, who's been given the "The Call," etc.

The Jobbers

Jobbers are to professional wrestling what the Washington Nationals were to the Harlem Globetrotters: They never win, and they serve primarily as fodder for the talent. There are basically three kinds of jobbers:

1. *Recent graduates of the wrestling schools*—Usually young and a bit awkward, these jobbers often have a different gimmick each week, while management decides whether they have potential to be talent.

2. *Part-time wrestlers*—Many jobbers work as prison guards, cops, bouncers, and even, yes, musicians. They pick up the going rate to do a match with an up-and-coming talent.

3. *Unfortunate individuals who think they're being groomed to be main-card wrestlers*—These guys never quite get the shot they're hoping for.

The wrestling business has a way of deciding who will get the push and who won't. Various factors determine who may someday become big stars and who will forever be the no-name opponents who get beat up on a weekly basis. Not always, but it's usually pretty easy to tell. The talent are suntanned, muscular, and wearing robes or costumes that sometimes cost thousands of dollars apiece. The jobbers are usually pale, nondescript, and in (reasonably) decent shape. If they have a costume or jacket, it's often something their wife has sewn together for them. Many of them are part-time wrestlers and full-time bar bouncers, security guards, or correctional officers. The standard pay for jobbers is around $100 to $150 a match in the big leagues and usually gas money plus $20 for local and indie shows. The jobbers' credo that I heard repeated almost weekly: "It beats the hell out of working for a living."

According to locker room protocol, the jobbers and the talent change their clothes in different parts of the locker room, and they don't mingle except to go over the match beforehand. Certain wrestlers have finishing moves that require extremely careful execution on the part of both the jobber and the talent. Jobbers are often warned ahead of time and offered extra pay to "take" a certain finish. An example of this might be where a jobber is hoisted piggyback by one of the name wrestlers and must sit stock-still while the name wrestler flies off the top rope and clotheslines the hapless jobber. The clothesline is supposed to hit just above the solar plexus—"supposed to" being the operative phrase. A bad hit in either direction can cause serious pain and even permanent injury. Of all the wrestlers I worked with, in many ways, I have the most empathy for the jobbers.

The Production Staff

The production staff consists of the directors and assistant directors, and the assistants to the assistant directors, and the interns who run around informing the talent and the jobbers of last-minute changes to the script.

The Writers

When there's a last-minute script change, the writers are the individuals whose job it is to give the wrestlers instructions.

The Floor Director

The floor director is the person who tells everyone else: "It's showtime!"

Planning the Finish

In every locker room, there's a separate room or area where some of the most important decisions take place. This is where the wrestlers, the referee, and anyone else involved in a match go to work out the basic progression of the match and, most importantly, how the match will end. Theoretically, a finish goes something like this: "Okay, you come out and go back and forth for a couple of minutes, then Wrestler A does a high spot, and B, you sell the hell out of it. Go back and forth a little bit longer, and then Wrestler C does the run-in, ref-bump, and Wrestler A you do the pin, but the ref doesn't see it. Finally, ref comes around, and Wrestler B does the roll-up, 1–2–3, and we go home."

In theory, this is how planning the finish goes. In actuality, this is where last-minute changes often occur and egos take over. Wrestler A is a name talent and knows that if the fans see him lose too often on TV, it may have negative consequences on his or her career. Depending on the wrestler's level of stardom or pull within the company, he may flat-out refuse to "put over" the other wrestler. Occasionally, the wrestlers will attempt to interject their own ideas of how the match should go. Sometimes this can get *extremely* heated, even resulting in ultimatums from one or both sides. Usually, a compromise is worked out, though on a rare occasions, Wrestler A will agree to the script and then change the finish during the actual match. This can result in some really, really serious heat and possibly consequences, depending on the wrestler's status in the company.

The Mania Seems to Work

As crazy and disorganized as it is, somehow the mania of wrestling works. Once the show begins, everyone stays focused on the backstage monitors. As the wrestlers finish their matches and return to the dressing rooms, they check to see how a particular move or spot looked on camera.

I was always impressed by the professionalism of "the boys." No matter what was going on in their private lives, or whether or not they felt well, it was an unwritten rule that when the cameras rolled, you gave 100%.

Television exposure was vital to a promotion but paled in comparison to the excitement of a live show—and that's what we'll look at in the next chapter.

11 GOOD EVENING, WRESTLING FANS, AND WELCOME TO THE SPORTATORI UM!

When you hear the word *Sportatorium*, you might picture a grand, pulsing arena. It was the scene of some of wrestling's all-time-greatest moments. In fact, the Tampa Sportatorium, located on the edge of a "transitional" neighborhood, closely resembled the 4-H pavilion at your county fairgrounds. The aluminum siding shook with every bodyslam, and there was a perpetual scent in the air—a delicate combination of Rum River cigars, stale Pabst Blue Ribbon, and bodily . . . I think you get the picture.

A Day at the Office

For a typical show, the wrestlers and managers would arrive at the Sportatorium about an hour before bell time. We'd go over the matches, get into our outfits, and go over the finishes.

Since I was the only full-time "heel" manager, I usually made three appearances per show. (By the way, managers never get in the ring during a match; to do so is instant disqualification.) There was a fairly standard format: I would flagrantly cheat and annoy the crowd to the best of my abilities for each match. At the end of the first match, the baby-face would almost, just about—damn it!—catch me.

In the second match, the baby-face would actually grab me, at which point I would begin pleading for mercy. He would hesitate a moment—long enough to be on the receiving end of a totally uncalled-for cheap shot from one of my "Flock." Then my Flock and I would get really mean and proceed to administer a gang-bang, gleefully kicking and stomping until the ref pulled us off him. Every now and then, we'd see just how far we could

take it and throw in a little blading action. It was hot in the Sportatorium, and even a small nick bled profusely. This round had to
be resolved fast, or it might push the fans over the edge and wear
them out before the last two bouts.

At this point, we might take an intermission. The fans would
go out to the parking lot and "fix" their Cokes, while others
would chat quietly with friends or total strangers. Which gives
me a good opening to express the following: A lot of people still
mouth some frightfully elitist platitudes about the wrestling de-
mographic. The truth is that nowhere in the world have I seen
social barriers crumble any faster than at an old-school wrestling
show. Hip-hoppers and Granny Clampett types unite in their
condemnation of the heels and admiration of the baby-faces.
("Someone's singing, Lord, Kumbaya.") People of every race,
size, and shape hold chairs, get drinks for each other, and play
peek-a-boo with babies while Meemaw gets a Marlboro. It truly
is, as the saying goes, "a beautiful thing."

Inspiring Crowd-gasm

After the intermission was a good time for a tag-team match.
A well-done tag-team match, complete with lots of juice, would
bring the crowd right to the edge. After that, finally, it was time
for the main event, time to cause the assembled fans to experi-
ence "the crowd-gasm."

Coming up with creative finishes that would produce a crowd-
gasm was usually one of the more fun and challenging parts of
my job. A standard second-match finish would consist of me on
my knees in the corner, begging for mercy, holding up a pill bottle and pointing at my heart, while crossing myself and taking
out my wallet, showing pictures of my wife and kids. Sometimes
this finish would expand to include a basic "power bomb." In a
power bomb, the wrestler would lift me over his head and then
hurl me onto the mat. I would remain motionless, spread-eagled,

for at least two or three minutes, sometimes twitching slightly to really sell it.

The night that The Nasty Boys returned from Japan, the final bout ended with an unscripted and painful finish. At the end of the match, one of them chased me around the outside of the ring, the crowd screaming for blood. I almost escaped, but then only three giant steps to the dressing room, a mere 6 feet from the Promised Land, he grabbed the seat of my pants. Next thing I knew, I was airborne, a human torpedo. My head made a direct hit, bull's eye, right in the center of the bank vault–strength dressing room door. I vaguely remember a dull roar. I assume it was the crowd.

When I came to, I was lying on a bench in the dressing room with a salty taste in my mouth. My scalp had been laid wide open and was bleeding profusely. I told you before about the practice of blading to obtain blood in the matches. There are also other ways (like ramming your head into a steel door) to produce the red stuff. When you get blood in such a manner, they say you "got it the hard way."

What's Up, Doc?

About a week later, I was still having some headaches, so I went to a doctor. I wish I had taped our conversation, which went something like this:

"So, Mr. Wirtz, what happ . . . oh my, you've got quite a nasty cut. That really could have used a couple of stitches. How in the world did that happen?

"I juiced the hard way."

(Silence) I think he was picturing an accident with a kitchen appliance. "Mr. Wirtz, are you on any mind- or mood-altering pain medications, legal or otherwise?"

Realizing that I had just used wrestle-speak to describe my injuries, I re-explained, in lay terms: "Doctor, I have two careers: I play music, and I am a pro wrestling manager."

(Silence) "A *what*?"

"A pro wrestling manager. You know, one of those bad guys who gets on TV and yells: 'Shut up, you bunch of genetic ("Please lower your voice, Mr. Wirtz") misfits, and let me, Rev. Billy, the genius of wrestling . . . ' You get the idea."

(Nervous laughter) "I think I understand. Now, how about the injury?"

I explained to the doctor the principle of the "crowd-gasm." He had stopped taking notes and was just sitting there listening, with a somewhat bemused look on his face. "So anyway, Doc, he grabs me, launches me 6 feet through the air, and my head takes a direct hit from the solid metal door."

"I see." He put on the rubber glove (just kidding), pulled out his flashlight, and asked me to look up, look down, blink rapidly; he checked my pulse, all seemed okay. "Mr. Wirtz, do you get cut 'the hard way' on a regular basis?"

"No, sir."

"That's good. Mr. Wirtz, the cranial area acts as the command post for most of your body. It serves a number of different functions. However, a battering ram is not one of them. May I beg you to try and come up with an alternate 'ending' for your matches?"

As he started to leave, I sensed that he was still trying to make it all add up. I asked him, "Is everything okay?"

Blushing slightly, he cleared his throat and blurted "I, I . . . I thought that stuff was all fake."

There are certain scenes, like outtakes from a movie, that stand out in my memory. Here are a few of them.

Starting to Make a Name

After a month of TV shows, Rev. Billy C. Wirtz, a.k.a. The Red Headed Geek, a.k.a. Woody Woodpecker, was starting to get noticed. As I was walking down the street in front of the TV studio after a taping, a Camaro drove by slowly, and an adolescent voice yelled "You suck!" It made my day.

Later that afternoon, when I arrived at the office, Mike was upset and unsure about how to handle a situation that had arisen. It seems that the part where I laid hands on my wrestlers and "healed" them before the match—à la Oral Roberts—had upset some of the local Christian folks. An indignant father had stormed into the office, accusing me of mocking Our Lord and Savior and such godly men as Jim Bakker and Jimmy Swaggart. Heaven forbid! I assured Mike that this wasn't the first time this had happened, although I was little extra careful getting into my van for the next few weeks.

Meet Billy Jack

Some 20 years after my time with the PWF, I clearly remember one particular night at the Sportatorium. The memory is especially clear during cold, damp weather, when I feel a twinge in my lower back.

I was beginning to work up some pretty decent heat with a visiting wrestler who had enjoyed a degree of fame on the national circuit. His name was Billy Jack Haynes, and his gimmick was loosely based on a movie character created by the actor Tom

Laughlin. The first movie in which Billy Jack appeared was a biker flick called *Born Losers*. In my favorite part in the movie, an innocent hippie girl (ultimately rescued by Billy Jack) was being introduced to the dastardly motorcycle gang The Born Losers. When they introduced a particularly nasty bearded character named Crabs, she asked, "Why do they call him Crabs?" The leader responded: "Because he's got 'em." Anyway, you can fill in the rest.

Billy Jack, an ex-Green Beret with Native American lineage, ultimately rescues the girl, setting the scene for the enormously popular sequel, simply titled *Billy Jack*. Prior to Walking Tall, it was the original entry in the "misunderstood good guy whom everyone thinks is a bad guy, until he saves the entire town from hippies, bikers, and lactose-intolerant lesbians" genre. It was also the movie that spawned the song "One Tin Soldier."

The wrestler Billy Jack wore a Hoss Cartwright cowboy hat with an eagle feather in it and was a "good guy" in the ring. After a few weeks of me calling him "a fat redneck," "Billy Jerk," and "a genetic misfit," he'd had about enough and swore to dish out revenge at our next live show at the Sportatorium.

Before the matches started, we were going over the sequence of events in the dressing room. Billy Jack was about my height and outweighed me by about 50 rock-hard-muscled pounds. His biceps were the size of softballs. We discussed how I would choke him with the cane when the ref was distracted and how he would chase me outside the ring and almost catch me. When I jumped back in the ring, I was to slip and fall, and then it was payback time.

Billy Jack was really quite the gentleman; he knew I was "green," so he kept the basic storyline pretty simple. As for the finish, he asked, "Do you know how to take an over-the-top rope bump?" "No," I told him, "but I'm a fast learner." He grunted and then, standing in front of me, he reached down and grabbed me in the "V" formed in the area where the leg attaches to the torso.

He explained: "Now, when I grab you here—and I'm not being queer or nothing—you jump." He continued: "I'll press you over my head, and you balance yourself by putting your hand on my shoulder. When I whisper 'neezow,' you push off, and on your way, grab the top rope and swing yourself over—that will break the fall."

I thought to myself: "Simple enough. Let's see: He grabs groin, I jump, he presses me twice, I push off. I grab rope, swing over the side, and land on protective floor mat. No problem."

The match was a good one. I gave Billy Jack a couple tremendous cheap shots with my cane, and he sold them great, rolling around and gasping for air while my wrestler distracted the hapless ref. Billy Jack finally caught up with me. He grabbed me by my red sharkskin pants, and I begged for mercy, the crowd howling with delight. He reached down, but unlike in his demonstration in the dressing room, his aim was just a tiny bit off, and his hand managed to trap a very small but very sensitive area of loose skin found in the lower region of the male anatomy. My scream of pain was not a "work." He pressed me over his head like I was a feather pillow, I reached down to push off his shoulder, forgetting that not only was he covered in sweat, but also, like many other wrestlers, he applied a light coat of baby oil before the match to lessen the chances of mat friction burns. It also lessened the chances of me getting a firm grip.

The next 10 seconds were a blur, but I vaguely recall sailing through the air, looking down, and seeing the top rope approximately 8 inches below my outstretched hand. Everything went black.

I was revived by a lukewarm liquid of some kind being poured on me be a jubilant fan. As I lay on my back, I noticed the foam rubber mat approximately 6 inches away from where I had executed an upside-down belly flop on the concrete floor. As I was hit by another drink, followed by a wadded paper cup, I realized it would be in my best interest to exit the immediate region—the sooner the better. Amid the now-familiar sound of 200 Floridians chanting "Red Headed Geek," I staggered back to the safety of the dressing room, looking like Otis from *Andy Griffith.*

Billy Jack was pleased. "Man, you really sold that move great," he said after the match as he gave me a slap on the shoulder, almost dislocating it.

As I climbed in the shower, I noticed an increasingly large red area forming along my floating ribs. By the next morning, an angry purple bruise covered almost my entire right side. I wore it proudly but wasn't bragging so openly about another bruise, much smaller but every bit as painful . . . in another place.

The World's Biggest Human

The PWF offices consisted of about four rooms. Two of them held desks, the fax machine, etc. One was the video room, where we would go over matches from previous shows and look at the demo tapes of wrestlers looking for work. The final room was a library that contained the entire history of Florida wrestling on film. I believe that collection now belongs to Vince McMahon.

One afternoon, we were looking at some videos when one of the wrestlers nudged me and muttered "Holy sh-t" under his breath. I turned around, and there stood the largest human being I had ever seen. His name was Jorge Gonzales. He was 7'7" tall, his hands were the size of catchers' mitts, and he was painfully shy. Jorge was an Argentinian, and Ted Turner had originally brought him to the United States to play basketball. That didn't quite work out, so they decided to make a pro wrestler out of him. He was there in Tampa under the tutelage of Hiro Matsuda. Of the many great trainers, none was better than Mr. Matsuda, who had trained many of wrestling's legends. Mr. Matsuda had been given the task of teaching Gonzales some basic moves, in the hope that his size alone would put him over.

It was a room full of men who all stood around 6'3" to 6'6", and Gonzales dwarfed all of us. I'll never forget the looks on the faces of the wrestlers when we watched him duck so he didn't hit his head on the ceiling. Unfortunately, Jorge's career never quite caught on. He could barely speak English, and unlike Andre and some of the other "giants," he really couldn't do much in the ring. He worked with both the WCW and WWE for a period of time before returning home to Argentina, where he passed away from complications due to diabetes in September 2010.

Cutting Promos

If you've ever worked in any form of televised entertainment or the motion picture industry, you know that very often scenes and/or scenarios are not shot in the order in which they'll eventually be shown. In wrestling, we'd do interviews where we'd verbally harangue the other wrestler prior to the actual show. These interview segments, known as promos, were often inserted right before commercials.

Blackjack Mulligan was a major country music fan, and he loved hearing about my experiences with some of the legendary players. (I actually played with Patsy Cline's original bass player in Winchester, Virginia, back in the mid-1970s. His name was Bill Bailey, and he often joked, "Yes, I did come home!") Anyway, Blackjack and I would sit there talking, and he'd be saying something like, "You know, Billy, I just don't understand how they can call Billy Ray Cyrus country music." The producer would interrupt, saying, "Jack, time for your promo." He would walk about 3 feet to our right, the director would give the action sign, and Blackjack would launch into something like, "Lemme tell you something, Rev. Red Headed Punk. You stick your snotty little nose in that ring, and I will break it off. If you even think about doing something stupid, you better fill out your last will and testament, 'cause you're a dead man." CUT!

Blackjack and I would pick up our discussion of why we liked Ernest Tubb more than Billy Ray Cyrus. I'd say something like, "Well, Jack, you know times change in music . . ." and the director would give me the sign that it was time to film my part of the promo. I'd step over to the camera, waving my cane and ranting something along the lines of: "Well now, Black Jerk Mullethead, if you saw what happened to (wrestler x) last week, you'd know what happens to overblown rednecks like you when they lay their hands on me, the mental genius and manager of wrestling champions. So stay out of my way, or you, too, will FEEL the power!!" CUT!

"So anyway, Blackjack, the country music industry, like everything else, is always changing. Hey, I'm going to run over to McDonald's. You want anything?"

Get Out of Your Gimmick!

Most of the wrestlers realized that the character they played on TV was just that. In wrestling, we called it your "gimmick." I was (hopefully) not Rev. Billy C. Wirtz 24 hours a day. Unfortunately, however, there were some wrestlers who were downright nasty 24/7.

During the time I was working with the PWF, I was also doing music shows around the Tampa area. One night, a whole gang of the wrestlers and their significant others showed up at one of the better-known clubs in Tampa. I was splitting the show with the Johnny G. Lyon band, the group that had been on the original wrestling show I'd worked, so it promised to be a "music meets wrestling" night of fun. Everything went pretty well for the first hour or so, and then during "Teenie Weenie Meanie," one of the wrestlers got into a pretty ugly altercation with his wife. When security told him to chill out, he proceeded to get even more out of control. I was onstage the whole time this was happening, but I was told that it took a total of six security guards to subdue the young man. After that, the club owner politely asked me not to play "Teenie Weenie Meanie" when there were wrestlers in attendance.

Lost in the Moment

I talked before about how I've taken nonbelievers to wrestling shows and seen them get caught up in the drama of the moment. One of my lasting memories is of a match that got a little out of hand. I don't remember the specifics, except that it involved Gigolo Jim and a baby-face. It was at a house show at the Sportatorium.

Somehow, whatever script we'd had went out the window, and the match turned into a full-scale brawl that spilled over into the second or third row of the audience. Normally the fans know to give the wrestlers room and not get involved, but that night, apparently it got to be too much for a couple of them to stand by and watch. I remember a large biker-type jumping on Jimmy, and without even thinking, I jumped on the back of the biker, knocking him down. What happened next was bit of a blur, but I do remember that someone took a swing at me, barely grazing me on the shoulder. I was about to swing back, and somebody grabbed me, not more than a few steps from the dressing room. The next thing I remember, we were in the dressing room, being admonished to keep things under control. There were a couple more matches, during which time I showered off and let the adrenaline go down.

Normally, after the matches we would walk to the cars in pairs, finding safety in numbers. That night, however, I guess I had my mind somewhere else, and I walked out by myself. I was reaching for the door of my van, and out of the darkness, a voice said, "Hey, Red!" I turned and found myself face-to-face with the fan I'd jumped earlier. I didn't even have time to get scared before he stuck out his hand and said, "Hey, I'm sorry. I just got a little carried away. You're good out there, man."

About an hour later, I was sitting in a restaurant where we often went to eat after the matches. Jimmy sat down next to me, and I told him what had happened in the parking lot. He smiled and said, "They love you." In music, I lived for the standing ovation and in comedy for that joke that actually got applause. At that moment, I was enjoying the hell out of being the designated "Red Headed Geek."

13 FROM BODY SLAMS TO BELLY LAUGHS

Every state has that road. It's a long, endless asphalt ribbon. It's unbearably boring in the daytime, and at night (cue *Twilight Zone* theme), it feels like you're in your own little spaceship. With the exception of the stars, the DayGlo instrument cluster in your rental car, and the occasional faded billboard, there's . . . nothing. Mile after mile, after mile, after mile, after . . .

In Florida, it's called Alligator Alley. As you ride along it, you're not sleepy, just intensely focused. Thoughts and memories of places and faces long ago forgotten begin to float through the void between flesh and spirit—the night you met Patsy Cline's mom, the same night when you opened for Little Jimmy Dickens at that really weird place in Maryland with Al Hogan. (Hogan . . . too bad he wasn't in better shape; he would have made a hell of a wrestler.)

I was driving over to West Palm Beach to stay with my friend Karen King after working at the Sportatorium. My side was killing me; those Nasty Boys had done it again. It felt like someone had used the left side of my ribcage for a Moon-bounce at a kid's party. As we insiders say when no one else is around, "Ouch."

Actually, I was having a ball. The Sportatorium wasn't exactly the Felt Forum, but from the tin roof to the piece of clothesline that separated you from the front row of seats, it was real. Back then, the great majority of the fans were true believers and loved to see me get tossed, spanked, stomped, and humiliated. By now, I even had a good entrance. I'd strut up to the ring, using "Sex Machine" as my theme song. Then I'd leap to the apron and attempt to vault over the top rope, into the ring. Unfortunately, my foot would catch on the middle rope, and I'd go flying, unceremoniously crashing into my wrestlers. Nothing like a good old-fashioned pratfall. It gets 'em every time.

Flashback

My first night on the job, as I was walking around the outside of the ring, I tripped over an elderly woman's foot. Having been raised "Southern," I said a polite "excuse me" and kept walking. Ten minutes later, damn if it didn't happen again. It happened a third time, and this time it sent me sprawling. Even before my vision cleared, I noticed something else: The unmistakable funk of whiskey, the kind named after combative members of the bird family and sold in half-pints. I looked up and beheld the angelic face of a senior citizen holding a cigar between all three of her teeth, cackling with glee as she flipped me (appropriately) the bird. From time to time, after I've eaten spicy food late at night, she still makes an occasional cameo appearance in my dreams.

Back in Tampa: Only $19.95 Plus S&H

I loved working for Mike and Steve, and I got along great with "the boys." There was only one problem. It was something I could no longer ignore, and it was getting worse, not better. The PWF operated on a less-than-shoestring budget. From the time I arrived until the time I left, I was told that a large financial boost was only days away.

Remember those late-night TV ads for "revolutionary" products like "The Pocket Fisherman" and "Veg-O-Matic"? How about "The Abdominizer" and "Crazy Calls"? Apparently, the PWF actually depended on such ads to pay most of its bills, but unfortunately, it just wasn't selling enough.

There were plenty of weeks that I let the PWF pay me whatever they could. I knew (or at the time, I thought I did) that I'd never have this chance again, and we were really beginning to come up with some good story lines. Mike and Steve, bless their hearts, did the best they could, but I was driving 13 hours each way, living at the Red Roof or the La Quinta (La Quinta being Spanish for "Next to Denny's"), eating a lot of fast food and losing a lot of money.

". . . and My Name Is Billy," Part 2

I stopped drinking on September 13, 1984. Unfortunately, after that, I developed some other problems. Thanks to a couple of accidents and a terrible bout with kidney stones, I'd begun using prescription narcotics for pain, discomfort, and, before long, almost any excuse I could concoct.

About a year before I met up with the PWF, in April 1988 to be exact, I again realized that the wheels were rapidly coming off my axles. So, once again, I walked into a room full of people with a similar problem, and once again, I got clean.

I'm not going to bore you with my drug struggle. Suffice it to say that I knew a successful recovery required daily attention, and (as I noted before) avoiding certain people and situations.

Sobriety, especially in the first couple years, presents a constantly changing set of challenges. It's tough to find like-minded folks, especially when you're on the road and by yourself all the time. If I got to town early enough, I might try to hit a meeting, but all too often, there just wasn't room in the schedule.

In Tampa, we had a couple of bar/restaurants that treated the wrestlers right. They gave us large portions of food, the waitress put up with our shenanigans, and often, they let us run a tab when times were tough. I felt it was important to hang out with "the boys," plus I really liked them, most of them. There was one night, however, when the inevitable round of shots got poured and one wrestler in particular noticed I wasn't participating.

"Yo, Rev. What's up?"

"Nothing, I gotta drive soon."

"Bullshit, don't be such a—"

"No, brother, I'm serious."

"What are you, one those alcoholic types?"

As the table began to get quiet, I realized that (a) he was really drunk already and (b) this could get very ugly, very quickly.

With my best "No worries" smile, I excused myself, saying "No problem, I'm going to shake hands with your sister's best friend, and I'll be right back." (At least one of the bartenders got it.)

I waited until my antagonist started chatting up one of the wait staff and slipped out the back door.

Later that night, driving to West Palm, I pulled over and checked my messages. On the machine was one from Creative Talent, the number-one stand-up comedy booking agency in the Southeast.

A Stand-up Guy

From the mid-1970s until the early 1990s, there wasn't a town of 30, 000 residents that didn't have comedy night at a local bar or motel lounge. If the town had a Cracker Barrel, you could bet it had a comedy club. Some of the places treated you like a long-lost family member, fixing you home-cooked meals and giving you a nice, clean motel to stay in. More often than not, however, the gigs qualified as emotional gladiator schools. Trust me, if you have even the tiniest self-esteem issues, barroom comedy is a bad way to earn a buck. Between the Jack Daniels–fueled hecklers, the horrible P.A. systems, the psycho club owners, and some of the terrifying motels where they boarded the comics, it could be a David Lynch movie come to life.

On the other hand, there was a lot of comedy work to be had. One phone call to Creative Talent could yield eight straight months of gigs. I was about the only piano player/comic on the circuit. I did lots of song parodies, nasty old blues from the 1930s, and some trick piano playing. It clicked with the right people.

I listened to the Creative Talent message on my phone. They said I was ready to move up the ladder and play the college circuit. On the college circuit, a one-hour show often paid twice what a week of one-night comedy clubs did. In fact, one Friday afternoon "happy hour" gig paid more than my entire stint with the PWF had paid to that point.

I had a choice to make. I could stay with the PWF, which I loved, until the bitter end. That end could happen in two weeks, or two months, but either way, there was no severance package, and some night, I might find myself outside a Legion Hall in central Florida, having to wire home to get gas money back to Raleigh. Or I could move on with Creative Talent. As I rode through the night, the choice became painfully obvious.

I pulled over in Yeehaw Junction to tell Karen I was running late and decided to call the PWF in the morning.

14 THE END OF ROUND ONE

After I talked to Creative Talent, I gave Steve and Mike notice. They understood completely, no hard feelings. However, this was wrestling, so there had to be a story line. I was the Red Headed Geek, and if I was going to get run out of town, there needed to be a pretty serious reason. I didn't like that look in Mike's eye.

Bite Your Tongue

It was the last match of my last TV show. Steve "Gator" Keirn was going at it with one of The Bounty Hunters. The Hunter knocked him flat and then started harassing the referee, diverting his attention. Meanwhile, I climbed in the ring and kicked Keirn in the ribs, hard. Then I knelt down, held my walking stick across his throat, and began choking the daylights out of him. (He later told me he almost clocked me for real; apparently my aim wasn't too good.) By now I was laughing manically, and with the announcers pleading for security, I stood up and "put the boots to him."

I felt a hand on my shoulder. It was The Terminator, who in real life was the brother of one of the famous Road Warriors. He was real big and real, real, real strong. The Terminator had watched me choking and kicking his best buddy, and now it was payback time. He nailed me with an open-handed chop to the jaw you could hear halfway to Orlando. Before I knew it, Keirn had grabbed me around the chest, The Terminator was holding me by the ankles, and I was upside-down. I heard the crowd screaming. Then the lights went out.

I'd just been on the receiving end of a match-ending move known as "the piledriver." For those of you unfamiliar with it, here is the basic piledriver:

1. Wrestler A (Steve Keirn) grabs Wrestler B (me).

2. Wrestler A flips Wrestler B upside-down. Wrestler B's feet are pointing at the heavens, and Wrestler B's head and neck are cradled between Wrestler A's thighs, about 6 inches above his knees.

3. Wrestler A drops Wrestler B, like a human post-hole digger, onto the mat, headfirst.

The secret to the move is that the thighs, theoretically, absorb the impact. Theoretically. Unfortunately:

- Steve was still trying to regain his wind.

- One of my shoes had almost slipped off.

- My head slipped through his thighs and *bounced* off the mat.

I was aware of a stinging sensation in my mouth. It was the end of my tongue. I had bitten off just a tiny little bit of it. Even in my semiconscious state, I realized that if I'd been making a face or yelling at the time, I could have very well been minus a very necessary and beloved part of my anatomy. I recall hearing the outro music being played. Someone whispered: "Don't move till the fans are gone. Man, that was great, you sold the sh-t out of that."

Apparently, it did look good. There's a TV monitor in the dressing room, and when the boys saw me hit, they were concerned. As soon as the fans left, several of them came running out. Keirn asked, "You okay?" He seemed relieved when I told him I was fine, just a little wobbly. We went out, had a fine shrimp dinner, and parted ways . . . or so we thought.

Postscript

About a week later, back in Raleigh, I was having headaches and tingling sensations in my neck. I knew a good chiropractor and gave him a call. He was running behind when I arrived, so a young, quite attractive nurse had the privilege of checking me in. I gave her all my vitals, and then she asked, "So, why are you here?"

"I took a bad piledriver."

(Silence) "You took a what?"

"Ma'am, do you ever watch TV wrestling?"

"You mean like Ric Flair and Dusty Rhodes, that fake stuff?"

Before I could answer, the doctor came in. He had on just a little bit too much $75-a-bottle-at–Macy's cologne, but otherwise, he was cool.

The nurse, doing her best to smile, told him, "I'm going to let Mr. Wirt-uths (close enough) explain it."

He sat down, and I explained, "Along with music, I work with pro wrestling. Last week, during the last match, there was a mishap. There's a move called the piledriver, and unfortunately, my head hit a canvas mat."

He held up his hand: "Wait, we're talking WWF—that kind of wrestling, right?'

(Oh boy, here we go.) "That's right."

"You got dropped on your head during a what?"

"A piledriver."

"Check." He paused, scratched his head, cleared his throat, and said, "I thought . . . " (here it comes . . .) "I thought the other guy was supposed to break the fall with his thighs."

GEEKUS INTERUPTUS

I loved Raleigh, North Carolina. I've been gone 20 years, and I still miss it. I made lots of great friends there, I cleaned up my act there, and in general, it was a nice place to live. But there's an unwritten rule in the entertainment business that if you want to get a shot at national fame, you have to move to New York, Los Angeles, or Nashville. Sooner or later, you gotta swim with the big fish. I picked Nashville.

Nashville

I was new in Nashville, and I was playing at The Bluebird Café, the top showcase room in the city. I walked up to the bar to get a drink. A fellow stuck out his hand and said, "You're crazy as hell, but I love your act. I'm John Prine." Do tell. It was him alright, and right then I knew I'd made the right move.

In Nashville, I also made friends with Fred Koller, who taught me the craft of songwriting. He'd written hundreds of songs, his best known being "Angel Eyes," which he'd co-written with John Hiatt and which had sold a few zillion copies for Jeff Healey. Fred and I were on the same wavelength in many ways, and I wrote some of my best songs with him.

I met a woman and dated her for two years before marrying her in late 1994. We'd been traveling around Florida on our honeymoon for about two weeks and were on our way back when I called home to check my messages. There was one from Steve Keirn. I'd been away from the PWF for five years, and I thought he might be wishing me congrats. Instead, he said, "Billy, I need you in Atlanta right away. The WCW is looking for new managers. I told them about you, and they agreed to give you a try-out."

My wife and I jumped in the rented Town Car and headed for Atlanta. We got a motel for the night, and I might have slept for an hour.

The Nature Boy

The next afternoon, I showed up at TBS studios, where they taped the weekly WCW show. The security guard made a phone call, the backstage door opened, and Ric Flair greeted me. Ric Flair? *The* Nature Boy?

My stomach knotted up and my hands started to sweat, but Ric immediately put me at ease. He politely introduced himself, his manner understated and businesslike. It was all a bit surreal. Here was the 10-time world champion, the most famous rant-and-rave interviewer in the business, speaking like a, well, like a personnel manager for Bank of America. He showed me back to the dressing room and told me he'd come get me in a few minutes.

While I was waiting, Mike Graham showed up. I was in the midst of thanking him and Steve for this huge favor when Ric burst back in the room, breathlessly urging, "Come on, come on. Let's go, we don't have much time." I was more than a little unnerved at what a hurry he was in, but then I remembered: "It's wrestling."

We walked out onto the set, to the podium I'd seen a hundred times on TV. The technical crew was setting up, but otherwise it was just The Nature Boy and me. He handed me a microphone. It wasn't plugged in, but he could still hear me. He asked: "All set?" I nodded, and he said, "Go."

I tore into one of my better routines: "Now listen up, you flat-headed snuff dippers, sittin' there in the double-wide with your toothless old lady munching—or should I say, gumming?—on a bag of Cheetos, looking at me, the object of every woman's fantasy."

Right in the middle of my harangue, Arn Anderson walked by. Ric held up his hand for me to stop. "Whaddya think, Double A?" "Hire him." Rick Flair told *me*, "You're hired."

We went back to one of the smaller dressing rooms to discuss my pay, the terms, how they reimbursed for travel, . . . Due to the adrenaline coursing through my body, I was fighting back tears of joy, having a hard time not jumping up and down like a kid at Christmas. Finally, all my hopes and dreams were about to come true. No more crummy comedy clubs. No more jerks yelling for "Freebird." I was going to be a somebody!

Ric told me to go on back to Nashville. They'd overnight tickets and fly me back so Eric Bischoff, the boss at the time, could see me and work me in.

My wife was waiting outside. She'd snuck in the back during the audition and knew the results. Standing outside the studio, waiting for the attendant to bring the car around, I was the happiest I'd ever been in my life. The rest of the day was a frenzy of phone calls, congrats from friends and family, choosing which outfits to pack, and another sleepless night.

Aside from the obvious leap in national stardom this would bring, there was an even deeper element of satisfaction involved. Ever since I'd chosen music as a career, I'd dealt with parental skepticism that had often escalated to openly expressed disappointment at my career choices. No matter what success I had, somehow it was always something that I should think about teaching a class in. Or, if I just had to keep playing music, it would make a swell hobby when I wasn't working a "real" job. Most of the time, it didn't bother me too much, but just the same, in the back of my mind, I was convinced that if I could just get on TV, the comments and "suggestions" would stop.

As I lay there in bed, I pictured myself on TV. Even though it was wrestling, which still didn't impress my parents, I was going to finally be a success, a somebody.

Oops

I got to the Nashville airport about two hours early, got a good seat on the plane, and rehearsed some of my lines again. I had a nice chat with the flight attendant. When I told her what I did, she was quite impressed and said, "I'll make sure to watch out for you."

I got to the Atlanta airport, and there was no one there to meet me at security, so I went on down to baggage claim. Still no one. I called the office, and after about three of four "hold please" answers, I got the message that someone was on the way. Sure enough, about five minutes later, I recognized a jobber named Joey.

I introduced myself, and of course, we were in a big hurry. It's wrestling. He snatched my bags, and we sprinted to his car. The car was in a no parking zone; Joey wadded up the ticket he found on the windshield and threw it away.

Joey had a Mustang but drove it like a Ferrari, zipping in and out of traffic, blowing the horn incessantly, drinking a protein shake, and telling me he was just about to get the big break himself and how he and Flair were running buddies. We pulled up to a traffic light, and taking a last swig from his shake, he opened the window and heaved out the empty bottle. It hit the pavement with a crash. I was mortified. People in the lane next to us were shaking their heads, but Joey was oblivious to it all, as he kept up his nonstop monologue. We got to the station, and he led me to the dressing room.

I found an empty locker and began to get my outfits out. I had my glitter jacket, a leather vest, and a really, really ugly blue checked sport coat, an obvious fashion joke, but quite the statement. I assumed someone would discuss my character with me before my audition. I was tucking in my shirt, talking to some of the other wrestlers, when once again, Ric Flair rushed into the locker room. Without so much as a greeting, he was literally pushing me: "Come on, come on, come on. Hurry, Eric's here, come on, let's go."

As we made our way back to the podium on the set, I grabbed the closest piece of clothing, the ugly jacket. As we were walking, Ric turned and said, "First thing: We need to get rid of that jacket."

Take one: Eric Bischoff and the announcer Gene Okerland joined us. Ric instructed Gene to ask me some questions and for me to do what I'd done in my interview the day before. Gene asked me a question. He was about 5'7", and I leaned over to speak.

"Don't lean over the mic!" Flair shouted.

Take two: Gene asked me a question, and I went into a rant—the same one I'd done the day before.

Ric and Eric began whispering. Ric stopped and said, "Okay, this time, do it without the comedy."

Take three: I did it again, without the comedy.

Ric threw another one or two suggestions to me, and I did the best I could. Eric remained stone-faced the entire time.

I stumbled through the rest of the interview, and Rick told me to wait for him in the dressing room. I felt miserable. But to my surprise, when I walked back into the dressing room, several of the wrestlers gave me a round of applause.

Gene shook my hand and said, "I'm sure we'll be seeing you around. That was great."

Whew. Well, maybe.

Ric came in and motioned for me to follow him. We went to a smaller dressing room. The Nature Boy cleared his throat and explained: "Listen, that was real good, but Eric just told me we're not hiring any more managers until after January. Don't worry, we'll call you." He shook my hand and left.

What Next?

I was devastated. I was furious. I'd never been more disappointed in my life. I'd failed. I was a nobody. I was supposed to fly out the next day, but I took a cab back to the airport, paid the change fee, and left that night.

I told my wife what had happened. I called my agent and told him I'd need some gigs after all. I talked to Mike on the phone; he guessed it was simply politics.

It took me several years to find out (one version of) what had really happened. It seems that at the time I auditioned, Hulk Hogan was more-or-less secretly calling the shots. If they'd hired me, they'd have had to fire someone who was part of Hogan's clique, and that wasn't going to happen. Apparently Ric had overstepped his bounds or was unaware of the power play involved.

My wife took me to dinner, my agent expressed his sympathy, and someone else mentioned something about teaching.

The following summer, I ended up touring with Boz Scaggs. Shortly after that, I had a speaking part in *Letter from Death Row*, a movie written by and starring Brett Michaels, lead singer of Poison. In April 1996, my wife and I moved to St. Augustine, Florida. Later that year, we separated, and eventually we divorced.

"Reverend, save me, brother!" The raspy voice sounded familiar, but I couldn't quite place it. "Hey, Rev, it's Kevin Sullivan. I need your help!"

Meet Kevin Sullivan

Kevin Sullivan was one of the most famous wrestlers in the business, especially in Florida. In the early 1970s, the first few years of his career, he was the ultimate baby-face. He was from a working-class Boston neighborhood and had overcome serious childhood illnesses by sheer determination and guts. Kevin made for perfect copy for the wrestling press.

Over the years, however, Kevin changed. By the mid-1980s, he'd developed a heel gimmick that was almost too successful. He adopted the character of a demon-possessed individual, going so far as to paint his face half-black and half-white, at one point even painting a Mansonesque swastika in the middle of his forehead. Abudadein, a mysterious figure dressed in a long black hooded robe and sporting a live python around his neck, would accompany him to the ring.

As part of his act, Kevin had mastered the art of doing the Linda Blair routine with his eyes while babbling "Satanic" incantations. His voodoo gimmick was so effective that there were certain markets where he couldn't work. I'd worked with Kevin in the PWF for a while, and during that time, we'd had a once-a-month card in The Bahamas. Unfortunately, many of the Bahamians actually practiced Voodoo. On several occasions, they attacked Kevin on the way to the ring, hitting him with sticks, throwing glass bottles, and at one point even attempting to tattoo him with a an old-style can opener. After the can opener incident, the Bahamian authorities refused to let him in the country.

Offstage, Kevin was an articulate, extremely well-mannered family man. Of course.

The Tonight Show with Jay Leno

Back to that 1998 call from Kevin. "Rev, we're doing an angle with Jay Leno, and I need you to bring a band over to Tampa tomorrow. Can you do it?" (Remember, it's wrestling, and 10 seconds to make a life-changing decision is par for the course.)

"Sure, Kevin, no problem."

I'd recently been working with the fellows at King Snake again, so I called Bob Greenlee and asked him if he'd like to be on national TV. Although it sounded like a no-brainer, at the time, Bob was getting ready to leave for his summer home in New Hampshire. Ron Foster and Warren King, the other two band members, were not major wrestling fans. Their main concern was financial. But they agreed, and the next afternoon, we packed up the gear and drove to Tampa.

When we arrived, there was the usual mass confusion surrounding any wrestling show. The first person we encountered was an ex-Charlotte cop, now turned security guard, who grilled us for nearly 20 minutes, demanding we take all the instruments out of the van for inspection, before Kevin showed up. The guard reluctantly let us in, disappointed that he hadn't found the 5 kilos of heroin he was certain I'd hidden in my piano case.

Kevin hadn't really had time to explain the entire situation. So as we set up our gear, he gave us some details. It seems that Eric Bischoff had worked out a program in which Eric and Hollywood (as he was now known) Hogan appeared on *The Tonight Show with Jay Leno*. While on the show, they got into some kind of verbal altercation with Jay Leno that escalated to the point where security forcibly removed Hogan and Bischoff from the set. America was stunned: Someone had actually insulted Jay Leno on national TV. What manner of evil, sociopathic cretin would do such a thing? This was a matter of national importance that could not be left unresolved.

There was only one man qualified to correct this terrible display of violence toward America's favorite comic: the master of the finishing move known as "the diamond cutter," my buddy Diamond Dallas Page. Sure enough, Page appeared on Leno's show and soothed his nerves. Then, just when all seemed to be smoothed over, guess who came barging onstage? Yep, it was the dastardly Hogan and Bischoff, at their most abusive, trash-talking best. Things got a little heated and a little more heated, and then an all-out brawl broke out. The net result: Dallas Page agreed to train Jay Leno to wrestle. Together as a tag-team, they'd take on Hogan and Bischoff at the annual Sturgis motorcycle rally. In the meantime, to boil the public's blood even further, Bischoff decided to parody the Jay Leno show on the *WCW Monday Nitro* program.

My part in all this was to provide a house band for the skit. Not only was I expected to provide music and play the part of the anti-Kevin Eubanks, I was also expected to write the entire script for the skit each week until the big match.

As we were setting up, I saw Bischoff for the first time in four years. Being the busy man that he was, he didn't waste time with "Hey, Rev" or "Nice to see you." He simply skipped to, "Are you going to make me funny?" Several answers came to mind, but in the interest of keeping my gig, I simply assured him that would be no problem.

All this took place with about 90 minutes until we'd be on national TV. Pressure? What pressure?

The band and I worked up a basic blues shuffle for the intro music. Then it occurred to someone that we didn't have a name for the show. I came up with *Nightcap* on the spot. So far so good. I racked my brain for some jokes and came up with a few stock club lines about Jay Leno's chin, his general appearance, etc. They typed them into a teleprompter, and, 3–2–1, we were on.

At first, the capacity crowd in the Sun Dome didn't quite know what was going on, but they soon figured it out, and by the end of the segment, they were loudly booing every bad joke. Eric gave me the wind-up signal, we played the outro music, and we went to commercial.

The Call, Continued

On the set of *Nightcap*, to our left, was the announcer's table. One of the play-by-play announcers was the legendary Bobby "The Brain" Heenan. On camera, he was one of the all-time great heels. For years, he'd been one of the greatest managers in the history of wrestling. He was a truly old-school guy. If you were "one of the boys," he was constantly joking with you and telling you great stories. If you were an outsider, he'd kayfabe you in a heartbeat. I'd seen him turn his back on many a fan, going so far as to them to f-ck off.

Following the skit, Bobby turned to me, introduced himself, and said, "Man, that was great. Did you come up with all that?"

It took a good 10 minutes for my feet to touch the ground.

If that wasn't enough, one of the assistant directors told me, "Eric wants to speak with you." He led me to a Winnebago/portable office out back.

Eric was sitting at a desk, typing out an email. Not looking up from his work, he said, "Rev, I'll need you every Monday night for about a year. Pay is $1,000 a show, plus transportation, and $250 apiece for the band. Can you do it?" Doing my best to not attempt a backflip in the confined area, I told him I could do it.

17 CARE FOR A NIGHTCAP?

I got home from that first *Nightcap* show, and even though it was nearing midnight, I called my cousin Hoppy, my friend SideShow Bennie, and my adopted brother Kenny Coble to tell them all the big news. I also called my friend Dennis Phillippi, a brilliant Memphis comic, and offered him cold cash to help me write good jokes for the skit.

Monday morning I called Eric's assistant. No answer, so I left a voice mail. By midafternoon, I still hadn't heard back. I left another voice mail. The next morning, I woke up and reached for the phone, expecting to hear the intermittent signal indicating a voice mail. Nothing. I didn't want to be too pushy, so I didn't call again that day.

By Thursday, I still hadn't heard from anyone. Our next show was two days away in Las Vegas, and I hadn't heard about anything regarding the skit, and no one had made arrangements for the band members' plane tickets.

Friday morning I received two phone calls. The first was from the secretary responsible for travel, needing names, addresses, and info for all the band members. The second was from Eric's assistant. I asked what direction he wanted the skit to go. He cut me off, saying that Eric just wanted some jokes about Leno, and he also wanted me to watch Leno's show and rework some of his jokes. Huh? Whatever.

I watched Jay Leno that night, and none of the jokes really seemed to have anything to do with Bischoff, or wrestling. They were mainly about Monica Lewinsky, but I did my best. I reworked a few of Leno's jokes and got a couple from Dennis.

The tickets arrived the next day, I called the guys, and we were off to Vegas.

Las Vegas, Baby

We got to the MGM Grand, checked in, and discovered that there was also an adult film convention being held there that weekend. This had promise. I sat in my suite and soaked in the wonderful feeling of being a long, long way from one-nighter comedy gigs.

I showed up backstage at the appointed time, copies of Eric's jokes in hand. Right away, I sensed that something was amiss. It turned out that we were lacking a certain permit. In Las Vegas, any use of pyrotechnics in an enclosed building required a special permit. At the time, Goldberg was one of the major stars, and his entrance consisted of standing on a platform while smoke and fog shot up all around him; it was indeed impressive, and an essential part of the show.

When I arrived backstage, there was a heated discussion going on between the WCW staff and the fire marshal. He didn't care who we were, and he couldn't have cared less that Time Warner owned us. We hadn't arranged for the permit, and if we used any pyro, he'd shut down the show. Period.

Our sound techs were several guys I knew from the music world. I asked one of them how such a thing could have been overlooked. He shrugged and answered: "It's wrestling."

By the time they came to some kind of agreement about the pyrotechnics issue, we were less than 20 minutes away from showtime. The road crew hadn't been told where to set up the Leno set, and Eric hadn't had time to go over the jokes, so they scrapped the segment. They paid us, apologized, and suggested that we enjoy our night off in Vegas.

From time to time, don't you get the feeling that the universe has a sense of ironic humor? I looked at the entertainment section of the paper, and playing right there, no more than 100 yards away from the coffee shop where I was sitting in the MGM theatre: the one and only Carrot Top! Scott (his real name) and

I were pretty good friends. So, after his show, I went back to his dressing room to say hello. Scott greeted me warmly. Of course, this was Vegas, so to complete this already bizarre evening, we were joined by some of his other friends.

Remember the convention I told you about? It turns out that Scott had numerous friends in that field as well. The "legendary" Randy West ([in]famous for a series of films titled *Up and Cummers*), one of his "actresses," and her escort joined us.

It was great to see Scott, and even though he was a most gracious host, I could tell he was somewhat distracted, doing his best to engage the actress in a discussion of the current state of the European Common Market (or something similar), so I called it a night.

Getting in a Groove

A week later, the next show was being held at the Alamo Dome in San Antonio—the single largest indoor facility I've ever seen. If you've ever been to San Antonio, you know that you could fit the original Alamo plus Santa Anna's army in the Alamo Dome and still have room for a Kiss concert. For our show with 30,000-some in attendance, they'd closed off half of it.

Once again, I had the jokes ready before I got to the show. Approximately an hour before showtime, Eric called me into his dressing room and told me to run over the jokes.

Before going any further, in Eric's defense, I must say that I've never seen another human being hounded so unmercifully from the time he walked into a building. He'd walk down the backstage corridor, trailed by a perpetual stream of wrestlers, production staff, and teleprompter techs, all firing questions at him. If you were able to get his undivided, or even semi-divided, attention for 30 seconds, you were extremely lucky.

When I got to Eric's dressing room, he was reading something, eating an apple, and talking to Dusty Rhodes. He continued to read while I recited the jokes. I'd read one, and he'd say yes or no. We followed this pattern show after show. After I'd read all my jokes, he'd say, "I need some more about . . . " This was where my job became interesting. Out of a week's worth of jokes, usually about 50% would pass, and then I had to come up with maybe a half dozen more in (if I was lucky) 20 minutes. Most of the jokes were modified versions of heckler lines that I'd used on a nightly basis on the club circuit.

Eric was a master at generating "heat." From his cocky attitude, to laughing at his own jokes, he was pretty damn good. He did a great job of being totally rude, obnoxious, and insulting to Leno. Once the fans understood the purpose of our segment, they greeted Eric nightly with a round of boos and catcalls that nearly drowned out the band. By the fifth week, they didn't even wait for him; they started booing when the band walked out.

Five weeks into the program, the bigwigs at the show bought me a $3,000 piano and got my drummer an entire new kit. They realized that it was cheaper than shipping our gear every week.

For 20 years I'd thought that getting on Leno or Letterman would validate my career choices and put me on Easy Street for good. So one night, I was sitting in the motel room clad only in my skivvies, watching Jay Leno. He was ragging on Eric when all of a sudden his onstage TV screen dropped down. Pointing at the picture, he said, "Look at his goofy band." There I was. I was on the Jay Leno show. By the time it registered, they'd gone to a commercial.

Backstage Rumblings

Backstage there seemed to be two schools of thought among the wrestlers and staff regarding our segment. There were those who loved the jokes and assured me that I was a shoo-in for a permanent position with the company, even after the conclusion of this angle.

On the other hand, there were old-schoolers who felt that the entire angle represented a turning point—and not a very good one—in the history of wrestling. Prior to this, beginning with Vince McMahon, there had been some use of non-wrestling celebrities at WrestleMania and similar events. However, up until this angle, outside celebrities were brought in as guest referees, timekeepers, etc. A few were brought in as guest wrestlers, but they were generally professional athletes or someone like Mr. T that the average fan could "buy" as being big and bad enough to get in the ring with the pros.

To the old-schoolers, Jay Leno represented an entirely different premise—the idea that anyone with even a little training could compete and actually wrestle. Many of them took this as a slap in the face, and I understood why. I could look around backstage and see at least a dozen extremely talented wrestlers who had spent years perfecting their technique and trying to make it big. Whatever the public wanted to call it, to them it was their life, their craft, and a matter of personal pride. These wrestlers were determined that every time they stepped in that ring, they'd deliver a well-told story and an exciting match. This Jay Leno business was an angle that negated everything they represented.

As the weeks went on, their discontent grew less and less subtle. As one of them put it, "I remember when we actually had wrestling on these shows."

I have to say that regardless of how some people felt about him and this era in wrestling, Leno really turned in a credible performance. There were no Andy Kaufman routines, and there was no foolishness. He took some pretty hard shots and delivered a few of his own.

Next Up: Sturgis

We did the Sturgis show in an unusually small facility due to the fact we were in the middle of the freakin' Dakotas. They put us up in a truck-stop/motel because the only Holiday Inn was sold out.

We decided to start the skit as usual, except that Eric would say something really hateful about Diamond Dallas Page. DDP would then run on the set, destroy all the furniture, and beat the tar out of Eric.

Eric told me he needed a really nasty joke, so I gave him one of the oldest (and crudest) in the world: "What's the difference between a '59 Cadillac and Kimberly [DDP's wife at the time]?" Answer: "Not everyone's been inside a '59 Cadillac!" It worked. Boy, did it ever. Page came out and went berserk. I hid under the piano, and the rest of the band high-tailed it off the set. The camera faded out on Eric lying unconscious beside what was left of the desk. So Leno and Page, with the help of Kevin Eubanks, defeated Hogan and (for some reason) Hogan's cousin, Ed Leslie (Brutus Beefcake), along with Bischoff. It was the last show.

The Party's Over

After the show in Sturgis, I asked Eric for a moment of his time. He was busy reading some sheet of paper but agreed to listen. I thanked him for the chance to work with him. I hoped that he still planned on using me for the rest of the year and reminded him of a couple of the skits I'd written for other wrestlers. The entire time I was talking, he never looked up. His carefully thought response was: "You never know."

I called Monday and left a message. The next morning, I woke up and reached for the phone, hoping to hear the intermittent signal indicating a voice mail. Nothing. I called and left messages Tuesday, Wednesday, Thursday, . . . Finally, 10 days after Sturgis, I got a call from Eric's assistant. He asked me where we were the week after Sturgis. As the anger rose in my throat, I told him as politely as I could that I'd tried to reach someone every day, and no one had returned my calls. He told me he'd get back to me.

About an hour later, he called back: "Someone forgot to call you." He added, "Since you guys weren't there, Eric decided to kill the angle."

"Did he say anything about continuing my relationship with the company?"

"No, but if I hear anything, I'll get back to you." CLICK.

I sat there and stared at the wall. They'd done it again. I just couldn't believe it. I called the guys in the band.

When I told them the "official" reason given was that "someone" forgot to call us, they were understandably skeptical and upset. Even though the novelty of being around enormous guys in leotards had worn off, we were getting weekly exposure on national TV, decent paychecks, and even catering privileges. In six weeks, we'd gotten used to staying at nice hotels and having family members tape *Monday Nitro* to show to all our friends.

After calling the band, I had the pleasure of, once again, calling my booking agency and then my record company. The record company call was an especially painful one to make because I had a new album coming out, and they were actually going to fork out the megabucks to advertise it on *Monday Nitro*.

I wracked my brain, trying to figure out what we had done. Why, if they know it was going to be a six-week angle, would they have told me they needed me for a year? I needed to talk to somebody who might have some inkling of the truth. So I called Moolah and told her, saying, "It just doesn't make any sense." To which she replied, "Of course it doesn't, sugar. It's wrestling."

18 WHAT HAPPENED?

When I agreed to write this book, I didn't realize that I'd end up getting some answers to questions that had nagged at me for years. But I've heard a half-dozen stories about what was going on around us in wrestling at the corporate level. I guess I have some inkling of what it's like for folks who get axed in company takeovers. I'm sure that after reading this, someone will come forward with some completely different information. But anyway, here's my take on what happened to the WCW in the years around the Leno angle. I've also answered the question of what happened to some of the important characters in this story.

The Game Changes

When Vince McMahon introduced WrestleMania, it set in motion a chain of events that no one could or would have predicted.

Beginning in 1985, the WWE introduced Hollywood celebrities, famous rock stars, massive sound systems, cartoonish characters with catchphrases, intro themes, dance routines, and other antics to the world of wrestling. Thanks to the WWE, the world of professional wrestling changed more in 15 years than it had in the previous 50.

In order to compete, the WCW was also forced to modify its presentation. The WCW copied many of Vince's strategies and came up with a few of its own. For a while, it was a dream come true for wrestling fans, especially on Monday nights, when the two outfits ran competing shows during the same time slot. Week after week, they seesawed back and forth as the number-one and number-two shows on cable TV.

The Jay Leno angle was only one of many the WCW tried during its final years. There were the dancing Nitro Girls, there was the New World Order gimmick, and for a short while, there was the Goldberg phenomenon. Since I started writing this book, I've spent many hours on YouTube, watching everybody blaming everybody else for the demise of the WCW.

Some actually point to the Leno angle as the beginning of the end for the WCW. But all gimmicks, theme songs, half-naked women, sophomoric humor, and less mentionable aspects aside, the main reasons the WCW folded were pretty simple.

In 1988, Ted Turner purchased Jim Crockett Promotions and renamed it World Championship Wrestling. For the next 13 years, under Turner, Time Warner, and, ultimately, Time Warner/AOL, WCW would go from being the top-rated cable show in America to being an embarrassing joke. The hiring and firing, the angles, and even the logistics were handled (and mishandled) by a succession of non-wrestling businesspeople, old-school promoters, and even some wrestlers themselves. What began as a quality product ultimately drowned in a sea of back-room deals, egos, and political backstabbing. As the old saying goes: "You can't let the lunatics run the asylum."

In 2001, Time Warner/AOL decided it no longer wanted to produce a wrestling program. Later that year, Vince McMahon, CEO of Titan Sports, bought the rights to the WCW promotion.

Where Are They Now?
I've mentioned a number of folks in this book, and most of them I've kept in touch with over the years. Others have come back into my life thanks to the writing of this book:

• *Steve Keirn*—Although I haven't talked with him in a while, I understand that he runs a wrestling school affiliated with the WWE.

- *Mike Graham*—We hadn't talked for a number of years until recently. Mike's doing finc and helped me understand the rampant confusion in the WCW during both of my stints there.

- *Mickie Jay*—Mickie beat back his cancer and lives happily in Key West, Florida.

- *Sir Oliver Humperdink*—Unfortunately, Hump succumbed to cancer a couple years ago. He was a great friend and mentor, and the world is a much sadder place without him.

- *Lillian Ellison, a.k.a. The Fabulous Moolah*—In 2004, I saw Moolah at the Angelica Theatre in New York City. She, along with several other women wrestlers of her era, were the subject of the documentary Lipstick and Dynamite, directed by Ruth Leitman. It was a well-done picture of what it was really like "back in the day." When I saw here at the premiere at the Angelica, Moolah was still Moolah. Apparently, one of the other wrestlers had made some disparaging remarks about her in the film. At the premiere, attired in formal dress, Moolah was still seriously threatening to "kick her damn ass, right here and now!" On November 2, 2007, at the age of 84, the queen of women's wrestling passed away due to postsurgical complications.

- *Kenny Coble*—My adopted brother, Kenny served as technical advisor for many parts of this book. Kenny runs an independent wrestling promotion in Memphis and remains active in the business.

19 THE "F" WORD, REVISITED

It's been 21 years since I made my first appearance on a professional wrestling show in Florida. Over the years, I've been a traveling musician, a schoolteacher, a freelance writer, a radio personality, and a pro wrestling manager.

Whenever I'm interviewed by the press, or even in conversation with other musicians and fans, inevitably they'll say something like: "Were you a wrestler or something like that?" I explain to them that I was actually a manager, and I'll sometimes even slip into character to give them an idea what it was like.

Of course, you know what the second question always is: "Isn't that stuff all (the "F" word)?" Over the years, I've answered it a lot of different ways and hopefully gotten them to reconsider exactly what they mean by the word *fake*.

Perhaps the best response to that question comes to us courtesy of my original role model. When questioned by a reporter who had recently seen him on a wrestling card, Ralph "Wild Red" Berry responded with the following unforgettable quote:

You have the temerity to accuse me of engaging in a fraudulent profession, yet you have contributed a portion of your insignificant substance to witness me perform. If you believe me to be a charlatan, but in spite of this, have paid your way into our world, then you, sir, are an unmitigated buffoon.

You have insulted me, but I will answer your question. I am not now, nor have I ever been, anything other than an honest, hard-working craftsman, engaged in a wholesome direction, for the edification and entertainment of the public . . . the public of which, unfortunately, you are a member.

I didn't get rich from my stints with wrestling. Thanks to the piledriver, I still get occasional twinges in my neck. And honestly, I still get a little bit sore about the way some of it ended. But ultimately, I don't take the broken promises and unannounced script changes personally. After all, "It's wres . . ." (Never mind, this is beginning to feel like a Foxworthy routine.)

Two decades later, I'm proud of the fact that I fulfilled that childhood dream of mine. For a brief time in my life, I was Rev. Billy C. Wirtz, Manager of Wrestling Champions, and I was The Red Headed Geek. I was a somebody.

A FEW WRESTLING TERMS

- **Angle**: The basic story line of a feud or series of matches resulting from an incident. Andy Kaufman's series of matches with Jerry Lawler amounted to an angle.

- **Baby-face**: The good-guy wrestler.

- **Blade, or blading**: The practice of using a portion of a razor blade to produce blood in a match.

- **Blown up**: Out of breath, usually as a result of steroids

- **(The) boys**: Any professional wrestler or someone connected with the business. Non-gender specific. "She's one of the boys" would be used to refer to a female wrestler.

- **(The) business**: The wrestling business in general. When we ask about someone, we say: "How long has he been in the business?"

- **Ceezarny**: A language used by wrestlers in which *eez* is inserted after the first letter of the word. For example, in Ceezarny, Billy is "Beezilly," carny is "ceezarny," now is "neezow," and business is "beezisiness."

- **Finish**: The conclusion of a match.

- **Gas**: Steroids.

- **Gimmick**: A character or persona adopted by a wrestler. Certain gimmicks included foreigners such as Nazis, Japanese, Iranians, and Arabs. One of the most famous persona was Ric Flair's "The Nature Boy."

- **Haircut match**: A match in which the loser gets shaved bald in mid-ring by the winner.

- **Heel**: A bad guy.

- **Hooker**: A wrestler with strong legitimate mat-wrestling abilities and an array of match-ending (or, in extreme cases, career ending) holds known as "hooks," often used to punish show-offs and those that don't follow the game plan.

- **Jobbers**: Wrestlers who never win and serve primarily as fodder for the talent. Even though they are at the bottom of the pecking order, good, experienced jobbers can usually earn decent money for TV matches usually lasting five minutes at most.

- **Juice**: Blood.

- **Kayfabe**: A term used by old-school wrestlers related to protecting the secrets of the wrestling business.

- **Mark**: A wrestling fan. Also denotes a wrestler appreciating another wrestler's abilities.

- **(Put) over**: Describes a wrestler whose gimmick the fans appreciate.

- **Shoot**: An event that's real. The rivalry between the Tea Party and the Democrats is a shoot. There is serious heat between them.

- **Smarten, or smarten up**: To explain to an outsider the secrets of the business. Generally frowned upon. Also a way of ascertaining whether all those present know about the business.

- **Talent**: The wrestlers and characters around whom a show is built.

- **Turn**: When a baby-face turns heel or vice versa.

- **Work:** An event that is staged or predetermined but presented as reality. The Jerry Lawler/Andy Kaufman angle was a work. Every wrestling match is a work. On very, very rare occasions a match will turn in to a shoot (see above).

- **PWF**: Professional Wrestling From Florida.

- **WCW**: World Championship Wrestling.

- **WWF**: World Wrestling Federation had to change WWE (World Wrestling Entertainment) after a copyright suit from World Wildlife Federation.

- **Stooge-ing**: Telling the secrets of the wrestling business to outsiders for personal gain. Does not refer to one who imitates Curly in public.

- **The Call**:Getting a tryout with one of the major national companies. Being called from the minors to the majors.

- **Stiff**: Making pre-determined moves appear "real" by making hard contact. Then opposite of "stiff" is someone who works "soft." A "soft" worker can make it look like he is ripping you apart, but is in fact. barely touching you.

- **A Typical Conversation Among "The Boys"**

Original:

Me: "Did you see *Raw* last night? That last match damn near looked like a shoot. (Insert name of wrestler) is totally blown up on the gas."

Wrestler #1: "Yeah, but that guy is over like rover. He draws serious heat."

Wrestler #2: (Standing next to a new girlfriend) "Hell, I mark for the guy. I hear you guys went to the Kayfabe Lounge last night."

Translation:

Me: "Did you see *Raw* [a wrestling show] last night? That last match looked like they were fighting for real. (Insert wrestler) has really been taking too many steroids, and it's beginning to affect his in-ring performance."

Wrestler #1: "Yeah, but the fans really like his character. They really enjoy booing and taunting him."

Wrestler #2: "I'm his fan, too. By the way, let's not talk about the wrestling business in front of my new girlfriend."

ABOUT THE AUTHOR

Born September 28, 1954, Rev. Billy C. Wirtz is a third-generation writer. His grandfather, Count Dillon Gibson, wrote the books *Figures in the Straw* and The Sea Islands of Georgia. His mother, Claudine Gibson Wirths, authored and co-authored over three dozen titles, including "The Llamas' Pajamas" for Humpty Dumpty magazine and Busy Toes, with Mary Bowman-Kuhn.

This is Rev. Billy's second book. His first, *Sermons and Songs*, was published in 2009 by Circumstantial Publications. His articles have appeared in numerous publications, including The Charlotte Observer, The New York Times, Florida Today, Musician magazine, and Keyboard Magazine.

Originally from Aiken, South Carolina, Rev. Billy currently lives in Cocoa Beach, Florida. He hosts a cybercast at rhythmrevival.podomatic.com as well as a syndicated radio program. He teaches and plays boogie-woogie piano.

Rev. Billy collects vintage cowboy boots and has a mayonnaise phobia.